JENNY McCOY'S

DESSERTS

~ FOR EVERY ~

SEASON

To my father, for teaching me to appreciate really good food.

To my brother, who inspires me to work hard to achieve my every aspiration.

JENNY McCOY'S
DESSERTS
~ FOR EVERY ~
SEASON

Foreword by Emeril Lagasse
Photography by Pernille Pedersen

RIZZOLI
NEW YORK

The White Beurré Pear

Oranger à fruits deprimés.

P. J. Redouté.

Langlois.

Augusta Innes Withers, delt.
1825.

P. Henderson 1819.

The Red Magdalen Peach.

Contents

FOREWORD

JENNY WORKED AT my New Orleans restaurants in the late 2000s as our pastry chef, so I've had the pleasure of knowing her for several years. There are many things about her craft that set her apart, but it's her passion, authenticity, and philosophy in creating desserts that has always struck me.

Beyond her years of experience in places including New York, Chicago, and New Orleans, Jenny shares an instrumental philosophy of mine in her dedication to using seasonal, regional, and only the finest ingredients. It is something most chefs would say is the key to making exceptionally flavorful dishes, and it is the foundation to how she created this book. Wherever Jenny's career has taken her, she has always been inspired by great-tasting and locally available ingredients. When she was working for me, she fully embraced the southern style, whether learning our traditional dishes like king cake, pralines, and banana cream pie, or canvassing the local markets for seasonal produce to incorporate into one of her often nostalgic creations. Fortunately for you all, you now get to learn her incredible desserts firsthand and bring them into your own home.

In this book, Jenny captures each season and the desserts that represent it best. She celebrates spring with a strawberry-thyme lemonade and blueberry-apricot cobbler and shows off summer with her plum upside-down cake and white-peach-huckleberry crisp. She draws out fall's finest with creations like pumpkin-maple ice cream and chestnut-chocolate layer cake and brings you the comforts of winter with an awesome banana pudding pop and dried fig and buckwheat jam bars.

Lots of folks can be intimidated by baking—the precision required and how you must follow formulas exactly—but Jenny shows you how to make exceptional dishes in an approachable and practical way, how you can bend the rules in certain places (and where you can't), and, my personal favorite, how to take risks. I think you will find that, like Jenny, her recipes are impressive and inspiring yet thoughtful and accessible. Her style is sophisticated yet simple in nature, and her desserts are sure to knock your socks off. Whether you're just starting out or a seasoned baker, I know you will enjoy this book.

—EMERIL LAGASSE

INTRODUCTION

SURPRISINGLY, MY FONDEST childhood memories of food do not include me in the kitchen tugging on apron strings. From an early age, I explored the culinary world with my family through meals at ethnic restaurants on Chicago's north side, encountering exotic flavors like wasabi (which my father mischievously fooled me into thinking was avocado), and weekend mornings spent indulging in local favorites, like pinwheel and butter cookies sampled from buckets at the Maurice Lenell outlet store. During a few holidays each year, my family would roll up their sleeves, sharpen their knives, and gather to prepare glorious meals, which ended in homemade cookies, cakes, and pies. Thankfully, many of those delicious dessert recipes have been handed down to me, and now I am able to share them with you.

The combination of restaurant dining, exploring specialty food shops, and feasting on special occasions set the stage for my love of cooking. Shortly after high school, an idea came to me during a Thanksgiving meal. My grandmother's table covered with our southern family's favorites—braised Swiss chard, corn pudding, and candied sweet potatoes—inspired me. The following week, I applied to Chicago's culinary arts school Kendall College. From a practical perspective, I figured if I liked cooking professionally, I'd have a job; if I didn't, I'd be able to feed myself very well.

A quarter of the way through cooking school I visited Kendall's pastry department classrooms. Blown sugar and chocolate showpieces lining the glass wall of the pastry chef–instructor's office were enchanting. I watched students ice and decorate magnificent multilayered cakes. From that moment, I became captivated with baking.

I immediately found a full-time position as a pastry cook at Gordon in Chicago under Chef Don Yamauchi and Pastry Chef Celeste Zecola. I loved the hard work and long hours of a fine-dining kitchen, and the camaraderie among cooks and chefs felt like a home away from home. The professionalism of Gordon's kitchen, peppered with the occasional profanity, was a perfect fit for me.

At Chicago's Blackbird, under the guidance of Chef Paul Kahan and Pastry Chef Carol Wang, I became schooled in seasonal cooking. Paul gave me a copy of a U.S. farmers' market guide and encouraged me to explore the fruits of the Midwest. I ate only heirloom apples and pears that autumn. The following winter, Paul granted me a week's vacation to make a pilgrimage to Berkeley, California, to dine at Alice Waters's Chez Panisse, America's most celebrated seasonal restaurant. By springtime, I had begun creating desserts at home, hoping they would someday be on Blackbird's menu. Soon Carol gave me carte blanche to play with any ingredient I chose, and come summer she honored me by including some of my desserts on her menu. I still treasure looking at those menus—variations on a few of my earliest creations are included in *Desserts for Every Season*.

While working in New Orleans for Chef Emeril Lagasse, I reacquainted myself with the recipes of my southern heritage. Passionate about seasonal baking, I used fresh ingredients from the Crescent City Farmers' Market for the

classic desserts I'd known since childhood. Sweet potatoes for my bread pudding were pulled from the ground just a day before baking, and I picked ripe Satsumas for chess pie and kumquats for marmalade from the trees in my backyard. King cakes were baked with local pecans for Emeril's Mardi Gras celebrations.

Then came the kitchens of New York City. Four days a week, en route from the subway to the pastry kitchen at Craft, Chef Tom Colicchio's flagship restaurant, I wandered through the Union Square farmers' market. Each season I delighted in the rich bounty of choices in the growers' stalls and hand-selected the fruits that made their way into my desserts. My recipe repertoire was given new and exciting possibilities now that I was baking on the East Coast.

The inspiration for this cookbook, which originated during my early years of baking at Blackbird, and was strengthened while working for Emeril, became a reality while I was working at Craft. In *Desserts for Every Season*, I share my years of experience making delicious, comforting seasonal desserts in professional kitchens. My recipes focus on the finest ingredients and are written in an easy-to-follow format.

MY BAKING PHILOSOPHY

A dessert should be simple in both preparation and composition. Understanding the distinction between a thoughtful dessert and a dessert that requires too much thought is my recipe for successful baking. Many of the desserts in this book are simple to make, requiring basic ingredients and kitchen tools. They are classics, with a slight twist of flavor or technique, that you will be proud to share with friends and family. Yet, some recipes are a bit more complex, giving more experienced home bakers new challenges and an excuse to purchase a special piece of equipment, like a doughnut-shaped baking pan.

Too many people believe that there are too many rules involved in baking. Baking my way allows you to break the rules. Following my recipes, you will learn my methods for doing just that. Should you accidentally preheat the oven twenty-five degrees too hot, don't stand around waiting until it cools down, just shorten the bake time, and keep a close watch.

When working with vanilla beans, some insist that the seeds need to be rubbed between one's forefinger and thumb with granulated sugar. I could never imagine spending time on such a tedious task. Peeling rhubarb or apricots is enough to make me go mad. There is just no need for these extra steps in the home kitchen. You will note that my recipes call for fresh lemon juice by the quarter, half, or whole lemon because measuring citrus juice by the teaspoonful requires more dishes to wash.

My favorite rule to break, which some bakers would consider blasphemy, is using nonstick cooking spray instead of melted butter to grease a pan. Cooking spray does a better job of evenly coating a pan or baking sheet and it's easy to use. Furthermore, it doesn't interfere with the flavors of a dessert.

But one rule that should never be broken is a commitment to using exceptional ingredients. When you start with perfectly ripe fruit, fresh dairy and eggs, real vanilla, and flour that hasn't been stored in the back of your pantry for months, desserts will taste better. It's that simple. Start with something good and you'll end up with something great—even if your crisp is a little overbaked or the cake topples over while you are assembling it. A scoop of ice cream or dollop of whipped cream will mask any flaws, and your dessert will taste just as delicious because of your extra attention to ingredients.

ON SEASONAL BAKING

Just because you can find raspberries at the supermarket 365 days a year does not mean you should eat them all the time. Most of us wait until Thanksgiving for an annual slice of pumpkin pie. This holiday happens to fall within the peak of pumpkin season. So why not live by this same philosophy throughout the year?

There are several reasons for eating produce in season, but here are the most compelling ones:

- Fruit grown in season, especially locally, is going to be the best tasting available to you.

- Shopping at the farmers' market will teach you a new culinary language. There is intrinsic value in the ability to ask a farmer which fruit tastes the best on that particular day: Which variety will make for a superb pie filling, or which is too delicious to be eaten any other way but raw?

- Absence makes your palate grow fonder. Choosing to eat fruits in season will help you appreciate them more. How wonderful is it each September to revisit crisp and juicy apples after they have been in hibernation for six months? There can be no question that the first taste of ripe strawberries in June is sweeter after a three-season wait.

Take a moment to explore the Seasonal Harvest Calendar (page 13). It charts the general growing seasons of fruit, mostly in the United States but also in tropical regions. This calendar serves as a guide to choosing recipes that are seasonally appropriate and for how to make smart substitutions. For example, if you want to make Warm Peach Hand Pies (page 198) when peaches are not in season, experiment with other fruits like apples, pears, or quince.

HOW TO BAKE MY WAY

Among my recipes you will find common ingredients like unbleached all-purpose flour and granulated sugar. Some ingredients may be new to you, such as buckwheat flour and sage honey. You will note that I use traditional techniques for steps such as melting butter and whipping cream. Throughout the book, I will teach you a variety of new methods, such as how to perfectly brown butter and make homemade crème fraîche. To help you navigate your way through some of the new ingredients and techniques more easily, follow these basic guidelines. You will be pleased with the results.

- **Read the entire recipe before you begin.**

- **Use the Resource Guide** (page 234) to locate ingredients you may not have in your pantry. Or ask your local grocer to order the specialty items you need.

- **Prepare the listed ingredients, or *mise en place*** (French for "put in place") first. In other words, measure ingredients beforehand.

- **Be curious.** If you find an ingredient listed that you've never used before, take a moment to browse the Internet and learn a little about it.

- **Take risks.** If you want to swap one ingredient for another, give it a shot. I can't take full responsibility for the outcome, but I'm certain you'll learn something new, which is the best method for becoming an experienced baker.

- **Make each recipe your own.** If you hate nutmeg, don't use it. If you want to include orange zest, no one is going to stop you. If you prefer more salt, then add it. Every time you create something from scratch, it becomes your own, so try spicing things up. But remember to be careful as you make adjustments. You can always add more, but you can never "add" less.

- **Find time-saving solutions.** Use nonstick cooking spray instead of melted butter. Divide the prep work into small tasks that you can accomplish over the course of two or three days. Purchase store-bought graham crackers when you don't have the time to make them from scratch. If you can find a way to prepare a recipe more easily than by following my explicit instructions, then do so. But try not to alter that recipe's character too much.

- **Be mindful.** Certain steps cannot be skipped. If a recipe calls for softened butter, it must sit out at room temperature until it is soft. If panna cotta needs to set overnight in the refrigerator, don't pop it in the freezer for four hours instead. Some steps just take time and are worth the wait.

- **And as a disclaimer,** keep in mind that some of my recipes call for raw or undercooked egg whites, which are not recommended for everyone. So choose desserts wisely, depending on who you're serving them to.

BAKING WITHIN THE SEASONS

THIS HARVEST CALENDAR will increase your understanding of baking throughout the seasons. It illustrates the peak seasons for each of the fruits used in my recipes, whether they grow in your own backyard or are shipped from across the globe.

I always encourage bakers to use locally grown produce whenever possible. But unless you reside in California (and even then I'd be hard pressed to tell everyone in the state they cannot have cranberry sauce on Thanksgiving), I find it impossible to live entirely by the "only shop locally" ethos. I will never stop using lemons just because I live in New York. However, you won't find me serving a lemon tart in the middle of July when bushels of stone fruit and bright green paper pint baskets filled with berries line the tables of the local farmers' market. Refer to the calendar to determine the peak times to purchase fruit from your local supermarket, too.

Note that the calendar is largely based on the growing regions and average harvest times in the continental United States. However, because many of us are lucky to have access to delicious and exotic fresh fruits and vegetables from all over the world, it includes some of my favorite tropical fruits that grow year-round in Hawaii and countries that have less noticeable temperature fluctuations in their seasons due to their proximity to the equator. You'll find the recipes that call for tropical fruits in the winter chapter. That is because I prefer to use tropical fruits to bolster my baking in the months when little more than citrus is available in the United States. And do not forget that weather conditions tend to vary considerably from year to year, and from season to season. These variables can speed up or delay a crop's maturity, making produce availability a little unpredictable.

Substituting seasonal fruits allows many of my recipes to be baked throughout the year. For example, a cake recipe included in the spring chapter can certainly be made during the autumn, or a tart in the summer chapter can easily be transformed into a wonderful wintertime dessert. When pears and cranberries aren't in season but you have a desire to make my strudel, consider another fruit listed on the calendar that has a similar flavor and texture profile—sweet yet tart, soft and juicy. Keep in mind that substitution takes practice to make perfect, but by exploring variations you will create original recipes of your own because baking is a craft that allows for improvisation. Trust your instincts when making selections. Decisions based on color, flavor, scent, and ripeness will create desserts that are divine.

So, if you live within a cherry-growing region, take advantage of the short season. Pack the family in the car and spend the day picking this gorgeous red fruit. The Cherry Jam Pie (page 131) will be the best you've ever had. Try a substitution—make my summer Peach-Buttermilk Sherbet (page 178) with the first crop of spring strawberries from the farmers' market instead. Or, puree a few overripe bananas from your local grocery store at any time of the year to make Banana Pudding Pops (page 84). Any way you choose to bake from this book—by following my recipes explicitly or giving them a twist of your own—you will surely delight in the results year-round.

Seasonal Harvest Calendar

autumn

	JAN	FEB	MAR	APR	MAY	JUNE	JULY	AUG	SEPT	OCT	NOV	DEC
asian pears	█	█						█	█	█		
apples									█	█	█	█
Concord grapes									█	█		
cranberries										█	█	█
figs								█	█	█		
pears	█	█							█	█	█	█
kabocha squash									█	█	█	█
persimmons										█	█	█
pomegranates								█	█	█	█	
quinces									█	█	█	
sugar pumpkin									█	█	█	█
sweet potatoes								█	█	█	█	█

winter

	JAN	FEB	MAR	APR	MAY	JUNE	JULY	AUG	SEPT	OCT	NOV	DEC
grapefruits	█	█	█								█	█
kumquats	█	█	█								█	█
Meyer lemons	█	█	█								█	█
oranges	█	█	█	█								█
blood oranges	█	█	█	█								█
tangerines	█	█	█							█	█	█

spring

	JAN	FEB	MAR	APR	MAY	JUNE	JULY	AUG	SEPT	OCT	NOV	DEC
apricots					█	█	█	█				
blueberries					█	█	█	█				
cherries					█	█	█					
plums					█	█	█	█	█			
rhubarb			█	█	█	█						
strawberries				█	█	█	█	█				
pluots					█	█	█	█				

summer

	JAN	FEB	MAR	APR	MAY	JUNE	JULY	AUG	SEPT	OCT	NOV	DEC
blackberries						█	█	█	█			
cantaloupes						█	█	█	█			
honeydew melons						█	█	█	█	█		
huckleberries							█	█	█			
nectarines						█	█	█	█			
peaches						█	█	█	█			
raspberries						█	█	█	█	█		
red currants							█	█	█			
sweet corn						█	█	█	█			
watermelons							█	█	█			

year-round

	JAN	FEB	MAR	APR	MAY	JUNE	JULY	AUG	SEPT	OCT	NOV	DEC
bananas	█	█	█	█	█	█	█	█	█	█	█	█
coconuts	█	█	█	█	█	█	█	█	█	█	█	█
lemons	█	█	█	█	█	█	█	█	█	█	█	█
limes	█	█	█	█	█	█	█	█	█	█	█	█
mangoes	█	█	█	█	█	█	█	█	█	█	█	█
passion fruit	█	█	█	█	█	█	█	█	█	█	█	█
pineapples	█	█	█	█	█	█	█	█	█	█	█	█

The White Beurrè Pear

Asian Pear Fritters
Pear-Cranberry Strudel
Fresh Fig Tartlets with Goat Cheese and Red Wine Syrup
Sweet Potato Bread Pudding with Crunchy Cashews
Buckwheat Honey Ice Cream
Honey-Roasted Pear Sorbet
Pumpkin-Maple Ice Cream
Baked Gala Apples
Black Mission Fig Preserves
Concord Grape Jam
McIntosh Apple Butter
Chestnut-Chocolate Layer Cake
Banana–Black Walnut Muffins

Autumn

Browned Butter Waffles
Jenny's Mulled Apple Cider
Hazelnut Brittle
Coffee-Cardamom Shortbread
Autumn Chocolate Clusters
Concord Grape and Rosemary Focaccia
Earl Grey Tea–Poached Pears with Figs and Pomegranate
Butterscotch *Budino* with Homemade Crème Fraîche
Quince-Apple-Pear Crostata
Concord Grape Ice Pops
Pumpkin Roulade
Persimmon Pudding with Greek Yogurt
Caramel Lady Apples
Pumpkin–Milk Chocolate Pie with a Gingersnap Crust

ASIAN PEAR FRITTERS

When creating this recipe, I knew I wanted something light and crisp, so I used a classic tempura-style beer batter to achieve that result. It pairs nicely with fragrant roasted Asian pears and cinnamon-sugar. MAKES 8 TO 10 SERVINGS

Nonstick cooking spray

6 Asian pears, cored and cut horizontally into ½-inch-thick rings

2 tablespoons plus ½ cup granulated sugar, divided

¼ teaspoon fine sea salt

¼ teaspoon ground cinnamon

Canola oil for frying

1 cup plus 2 tablespoons unbleached all-purpose flour

1 cup cornstarch

One 12-ounce bottle of beer (preferably a lager or pilsner)

POSITION A RACK in the center of the oven and preheat to 350°F. Lightly coat a baking sheet with nonstick cooking spray.

In a large bowl, gently toss the pear rings with 2 tablespoons of the sugar and the salt, until coated. Lay the slices of pear in a single layer on the prepared baking sheet and roast for 8 minutes. Flip the slices over and continue to roast until the pears are just tender, 6 to 8 more minutes. Place the pears in the refrigerator to cool to room temperature.

Line a baking sheet or large platter with paper towels. Toss the remaining ½ cup sugar and the cinnamon in a medium bowl and set aside. Fill a large skillet about 2 inches deep with oil. Heat over medium heat until the oil reaches 350°F on a deep-frying thermometer.

In a large bowl, whisk the flour and cornstarch together. Slowly add the beer, whisking constantly, and mix until perfectly smooth. Dip 6 pear slices in the batter, taking care to completely coat each slice, and quickly drop them into the hot oil. Fry until crisp and light golden brown, about 2 minutes on each side. Remove the slices with chopsticks or a slotted spoon and transfer to the paper towels to drain. Repeat with the remaining pear slices. While warm, toss the slices in the cinnamon-sugar and serve immediately. Discard any remaining batter.

PEAR-CRANBERRY STRUDEL

I became a strudel connoisseur during a trip to Vienna with my mother. Every morning begun with a strong *kaffee* and a strudel. The afternoon snack included another *kaffee* and a strudel. And, of course, each evening ended with a *kaffee* and a strudel. My recipe, unlike the traditional Austrian version, calls for the use of phyllo dough instead of strudel dough, a much more manageable method for making this homemade pastry, but just as good. MAKES 12 SERVINGS

6 ripe Bartlett Pears

Finely grated zest of ½ lemon

½ teaspoon fine sea salt

¾ cup packed light brown sugar

¾ teaspoon ground cinnamon, plus more for topping

4½ ounces (9 tablespoons) unsalted butter, divided

¾ cup cranberries, sliced in half

12 sheets (about 6 ounces) fresh or frozen phyllo dough, thawed

Granulated sugar

1 tablespoon turbinado sugar

POSITION A RACK in the center of the oven and preheat to 350°F. Cover a large, flat work surface with 2 sheets of parchment paper. Line a baking sheet with parchment paper.

Peel, core, and dice the pears into ¼-inch cubes. Gently toss the pears, lemon zest, salt, brown sugar, and cinnamon in a large bowl until evenly combined.

In a large sauté pan, melt 1 tablespoon of the butter. Add the pear mixture and cook over high heat until just softened. Using a slotted spoon, transfer the pears to a shallow dish and discard the excess liquid. Let cool to room temperature. Transfer the mixture to a bowl, add the cranberries, gently stir to combine, and set aside.

Place the stack of phyllo sheets on one of the sheets of parchment that is on your work surface and cover with plastic wrap to prevent the phyllo dough from drying out. In a small saucepan, melt the remaining 8 tablespoons butter over low heat.

Arrange 1 sheet of phyllo on the second sheet of parchment, with the long side of the sheet parallel to the edge of the work surface. Lightly brush the entire surface area of the phyllo with melted butter, starting from the center of the sheet and working outward to prevent tears *(fig. 1)*. Lightly sprinkle the entire sheet of phyllo evenly with a few pinches of granulated sugar and top with another sheet of phyllo, taking care to line up the corners of each layer. Brush with melted butter, sprinkle with granulated sugar, and repeat with 2 more sheets of phyllo to create a four-layer stack.

Using a pizza wheel, and the straight edge of a ruler as a guide, cut the buttered and sugared phyllo stack in half widthwise. Then cut the 2 pieces in half again, creating 4 strips *(fig. 2)*. About 2 inches from the bottom edges of the 4 strips, evenly divide one-third of the pear-cranberry filling *(fig. 3)*, fold the edge over the filling, and tightly roll up *(figs. 4 and 5)*. Lightly brush the entire exterior surface of the rolled strudel with melted butter and sprinkle the tops of the assembled strudel generously with turbinado sugar and ground cinnamon *(fig. 6)*. Repeat two more times with the remaining 8 sheets of phyllo and the remaining two-thirds of the pear-cranberry filling to make 8 more strudels.

Sprinkle the tops of the assembled strudels generously with turbinado sugar and cinnamon and bake until golden brown, 35 to 40 minutes. Serve warm.

FRESH FIG TARTLETS WITH GOAT CHEESE AND RED WINE SYRUP

At Craft in New York City, I worked alongside the celebrated American pastry chef Claudia Fleming on the night of the restaurant's tenth anniversary. When we couldn't decide on our special dessert collaboration, we invited guests to create their own grand finale. We covered the tables with bowls filled with mousse, platters of fruit, and cake stands piled with tart shells. The final course was spectacular, and my Blonde Sablé Dough tartlet filled with Claudia's goat cheese cream, fresh figs from Long Island's North Fork, and a simple red wine syrup was my favorite combination. Here is my version of this memorable dessert. MAKES 10 TO 12 TARTLETS

Nonstick cooking spray

Unbleached all-purpose
flour for dusting

1 recipe Blonde Sablé Dough
(page 224)

1 cup (4 ounces) fresh
goat cheese

1 cup (4 ounces) mascarpone

1 cup heavy cream

½ cup confectioners' sugar

Finely grated zest of ½ orange

24 ripe Black Mission or
Calimyrna figs

1 recipe Red Wine Syrup
(recipe follows)

LINE TWO BAKING sheets with parchment paper. Lightly coat a 12-cavity muffin pan with nonstick cooking spray.

On a lightly floured surface, roll one disk of chilled dough into a large rectangle by starting at the center of the disk and rolling away from you. Use additional flour and give the dough a quarter turn between each roll to prevent it from sticking to the table. Continue rolling until the dough is an even ⅛ inch thick. Drape the dough over the rolling pin, transfer to a prepared baking sheet, and refrigerate for about 30 minutes. Repeat with the second disk of dough.

Once the sheets of dough are firm, cut 5-inch circles from the dough and carefully line each muffin cavity with 1 circle of dough, pressing the dough evenly into the interior corners and gently pressing folds against the sides of the cavities of the pan. Freeze the lined muffin pan until the dough is fully hardened, about 15 minutes.

Position a rack in the center of the oven and preheat to 350°F. Fit a pastry bag with a ½-inch round pastry tip.

Bake the shells until light golden brown, 16 to 18 minutes. Rotate the muffin pan midway through the baking time and pierce the dough gently with a fork if the centers of the shells puff up. Let cool to room temperature.

In the bowl of a stand mixer fitted with the paddle attachment, cream the goat cheese, mascarpone, cream, confectioners' sugar, and orange zest on

medium speed until thickened and smooth, 3 to 5 minutes. Transfer the mixture to the prepared pastry bag and refrigerate until ready to use.

About 30 minutes before serving, pipe the goat cheese filling into each tart shell until full. Trim the stems from the figs and cut the figs into quarters. Gently toss the figs in about half of the syrup to coat. Top each tart with figs and drizzle with the remaining syrup just before serving.

Red Wine Syrup

¾ cup red wine

¾ cup granulated sugar

Finely grated zest of ¼ orange

1 cinnamon stick

3 whole star anise

6 whole cloves

¼ teaspoon pink peppercorns

¼ teaspoon black peppercorns

¼ teaspoon whole
coriander seeds

½ teaspoon whole allspice

IN A SMALL saucepan, bring the wine, sugar, orange zest, cinnamon, star anise, cloves, pink peppercorns, black peppercorns, coriander, and allspice to a boil and cook until the liquid is reduced by about half. Strain the syrup through a fine-mesh sieve into a bowl and let cool to room temperature. Discard the spices.

SWEET POTATO BREAD PUDDING WITH CRUNCHY CASHEWS

My friend Jessica Cutter, a former pastry chef for Emeril, shared the recipe for this twist on New Orleans's most well-known dessert with me. Over the years I've adapted it by adding cashews as a crunchy topping. MAKES 8 TO 10 SERVINGS

2 pounds sweet potatoes

1 cup whole milk, divided

4 large eggs

¼ cup granulated sugar

½ cup packed dark brown sugar

¾ teaspoon fine sea salt

¾ teaspoon pure vanilla extract

1 tablespoon plus 2 teaspoons whiskey

Finely grated zest of ¼ orange

½ teaspoon ground cinnamon

½ teaspoon ground nutmeg

¼ teaspoon ground ginger

¼ teaspoon ground allspice

1 cup heavy cream

6 cups (about 8 ounces) soft white bread cut into ¾-inch cubes

Nonstick cooking spray

½ cup (about 2½ ounces) whole cashews, roughly chopped

1 tablespoon turbinado sugar

POSITION A RACK in the center of the oven and preheat to 375°F.

Wrap the sweet potatoes individually in aluminum foil. Place them on a baking sheet and bake until soft when pierced with a fork, 1 to 1½ hours. Let cool until just warm. Remove the foil, cut the potatoes in half, and scoop the flesh from the skins. Transfer the cooked sweet potato to a food processor, add ½ cup of the milk, and process until smooth.

In a large bowl, whisk the eggs, granulated sugar, brown sugar, salt, vanilla, whiskey, orange zest, cinnamon, nutmeg, ginger, and allspice together until smooth. Meanwhile, bring the remaining ½ cup milk and the cream to a boil in a small saucepan. Slowly pour the hot cream over the egg mixture, whisking constantly. Add the sweet potato puree and stir until evenly combined. Add the bread and gently stir to combine. Refrigerate the bread pudding base for at least 2 hours and up to overnight.

Position a rack in the center of the oven and preheat to 350°F. Lightly coat a 9-inch square baking pan with nonstick cooking spray.

Stir the bread pudding base, then pour it into the prepared baking dish. Sprinkle the top with the cashews and turbinado sugar and bake until golden brown, slightly puffed, and set, 35 to 40 minutes. Serve warm or at room temperature.

NOTE: For a novel twist inspired by the traditional Thanksgiving side dish candied sweet potatoes, serve each slice of this dessert with a generous dollop of my toasted marshmallow meringue (see page 191).

BUCKWHEAT HONEY ICE CREAM

Chef Paul Kahan of Chicago's Blackbird introduced me to my first taste of buckwheat honey. My initial instinct was to spit it out: My twenty-year-old palate was not ready for this very distinct flavor. But over that autumn season, as I spun batch after batch of this ice cream, I acquired an everlasting love for the sweet, yet savory, bite of buckwheat honey. MAKES I QUART

7 large egg yolks

1½ cups whole milk

1½ cups heavy cream

¼ teaspoon fine sea salt

2 tablespoons granulated sugar

½ cup buckwheat honey, plus additional for drizzling (optional)

1 recipe Caramel Sauce (page 228; optional)

PREPARE A LARGE bowl of ice water and set aside. Put the egg yolks in a large heatproof bowl and set aside.

In a medium saucepan, bring the milk, cream, and salt to a rolling boil. Whisk the sugar into the egg yolks until smooth. Slowly pour the hot cream mixture over the yolks, whisking constantly. When completely combined, add the honey and whisk until dissolved. Strain the mixture through a fine-mesh sieve into a large, clean heatproof bowl. Place the bowl of ice-cream base in the prepared bowl of ice water and stir until cool.

Freeze the mixture in an ice-cream machine according to the manufacturer's directions until the ice cream has a smooth, soft-serve-like texture. Store in the freezer for 4 hours to harden. Drizzle buckwheat honey or Caramel Sauce (if using) over the ice cream.

(clockwise from top left) Buckwheat Honey Ice Cream, Honey-Roasted Pear Sorbet, Pumpkin-Maple Ice Cream

HONEY-ROASTED PEAR SORBET

I don't want the neighbors calling the firehouse when you make this recipe, but don't be alarmed if a bit of smoke billows from the fruit when you remove it from the oven. To ensure a rich, caramelized flavor from the roasted pears, let them bake until they are nearly burned to a crisp on the edges. Once the pears are pureed, the blackened bits will mellow, creating a fragrant and delicious sorbet. MAKES I QUART

Nonstick cooking spray

5 to 6 ripe Bartlett pears

½ cup honey, divided

1¾ cups water

¼ teaspoon fine sea salt

½ cup granulated sugar

Juice of ½ lemon

POSITION A RACK in the center of the oven and preheat to 450°F. Lightly coat a 9 by 13-inch baking dish with nonstick cooking spray. Prepare a large bowl of ice water and set aside.

Core the pears and chop into ½-inch pieces, keeping the skin on the fruit. Toss the pears and ¼ cup of the honey in a bowl until evenly coated. Spread the pears evenly in the prepared baking dish and roast until deep golden brown and the edges begin to burn, about 30 minutes. Remove from the oven and let stand for 5 minutes.

Transfer the roasted pears to a blender. Add the remaining ¼ cup honey, the water, salt, sugar, and lemon juice and puree until perfectly smooth. Strain the mixture through a fine-mesh sieve into a bowl. Place the bowl of sorbet base over the prepared bowl of ice water and stir until cool.

Process the mixture in an ice-cream machine according to the manufacturer's directions until the sorbet has a smooth, creamy texture. Store in the freezer for 4 hours to set before serving.

PUMPKIN-MAPLE ICE CREAM

As the weather becomes chillier, I like to make a batch of Pumpkin-Maple Ice Cream to help transition my palate from summer's refreshing melons and light desserts into autumn's hearty apples, pears, and pumpkins. MAKES I QUART

7 large egg yolks

1 cup pure maple syrup, preferably grade B

1½ cups whole milk

1½ cups heavy cream

¼ teaspoon fine sea salt

¼ teaspoon ground cinnamon

Generous pinch of ground ginger

Generous pinch of ground nutmeg

¾ cup Roasted Sugar Pumpkin and Kabocha Squash (page 233)

PREPARE A LARGE bowl of ice water and set aside. Place the egg yolks in a large bowl and set aside.

In a medium saucepan, simmer the syrup until it is reduced by half. Add the milk, cream, salt, cinnamon, ginger, nutmeg, and roasted pumpkin and squash and bring to a boil. Slowly pour the hot cream mixture over the yolks, whisking constantly, until completely combined. Strain the mixture through a fine-mesh sieve into a large heatproof bowl. Place the bowl of ice-cream base over the prepared bowl of ice water and stir until cool.

Freeze the mixture in an ice-cream machine according to the manufacturer's directions until the ice cream has a smooth, soft-serve-like texture. Store in the freezer for 4 hours to set before serving.

Grade B maple syrup makes all the difference for this recipe. It is a less-refined variety, so it has a stronger flavor and darker color–perfect for dessert. However, it can be a challenge to find if you live far from where maple syrup is produced. My favorite source for grade B maple syrup is Coombs Family Farms (see Resource Guide, page 234).

BAKED GALA APPLES

Mothers and daughters often disagree, and my mother and I were no exception. But, when it came to apples, we agreed that cooked—with butter, sugar, and spices—is much better than raw. Mom taught me how to make these simple baked apples, which are hollowed out, stuffed with cinnamon-raisin filling, and baked until just tender.

MAKES 8 SERVINGS

8 medium Gala apples

4 ounces (1 stick) unsalted butter, softened

½ cup packed dark brown sugar

1 cup raisins, divided

Seeds from ½ vanilla bean

½ teaspoon ground cinnamon

½ teaspoon fine sea salt

POSITION A RACK in the center of the oven and preheat to 375°F.

Slice the tops off the apples, about ¾ inch thick, keeping the stems intact; set aside. Using a large melon baller, scoop out the core of each apple, taking care not to create a hole in the bottom of the apple.

In a medium bowl, stir together the butter, brown sugar, ½ cup of the raisins, the vanilla, cinnamon, and salt until evenly combined. Pack the core of each apple full with the raisin filling, reserving the extra for later use. Replace the tops of the apples and place the apples in a large baking dish. Fill the baking dish with about ¼ inch of water, cover with aluminum foil, and bake for 15 minutes. Remove the dish from the oven, poke several large holes in the foil, and continue to bake until the apples are fork tender, 10 to 15 minutes.

Combine the remaining raisin filling and ½ cup raisins in a small saucepan. Simmer over low heat until the raisins have just softened. Just before serving, spoon warm raisin sauce over the apples.

BLACK MISSION FIG PRESERVES

This preserve is a favorite because it combines the flavors of rich cooked figs with the lightness of fresh figs. For a turnover, I spread this preserve in between puff pastry. I also use it as a layer cake filling, a topping for a panna cotta, and even enjoy it straight from the jar. MAKES 3 CUPS

1 tablespoon plus ¼ cup granulated sugar, divided

¼ teaspoon powdered pectin

1½ pounds ripe Black Mission figs, divided

¼ teaspoon fine sea salt

¼ cup packed light brown sugar

Juice of 1 orange

¼ teaspoon balsamic vinegar

IN A SMALL bowl, whisk together 1 tablespoon of the granulated sugar and the pectin and set aside. Trim the stems from the figs, and cut the figs into eighths.

In a medium saucepan, bring about two-thirds of the figs, the salt, brown sugar, orange juice, vinegar, and the remaining ¼ cup granulated sugar to a boil, stirring frequently. Reduce the heat to a simmer and cook until the figs are soft, darkened in color, and the liquid begins to thicken, about 15 minutes. Add the sugar and pectin mixture, stir until fully dissolved, and cook for another 3 minutes. Remove from the heat, add the remaining figs, and let cool to room temperature. Serve immediately or refrigerate until ready to eat.

NOTE: Since this recipe calls for fresh figs, it doesn't contain enough sugar to make it suitable for canning. However, you can still store the preserves in pretty little glass jars as long as they are kept refrigerated for up to 5 days.

(clockwise from top left) Black Mission Fig Preserves, Concord Grape Jam, McIntosh Apple Butter

CONCORD GRAPE JAM

Concord grape is one of the quintessential flavors of an American childhood. Many of us grew up eating peanut butter sandwiches, slathered with copious spoonfuls of grape jelly—and that jelly just so happened to be made with one of autumn's best bounties, Concord grapes. My recipe has the ever-popular flavor of Concord grape jelly, but is even more intense because I have pureed the skins of the grapes, giving it a heartier and more satisfying texture. MAKES 1½ CUPS

1 pound Concord grapes, stems removed

1 tablespoon plus ½ cup granulated sugar, divided

¾ teaspoon powdered pectin

Pinch of fine sea salt

PEEL THE SKINS from the grapes, place the skins in a blender, and set aside. Stir 1 tablespoon of the sugar and the pectin together in a small bowl until evenly combined; set aside.

Combine the interior flesh of the grapes, ¼ cup of the remaining sugar, and the salt in a small saucepan and simmer until the grapes have softened, about 5 minutes. Strain the grape mixture through a fine-mesh sieve into a bowl and, using a rubber spatula, push all of the grape flesh through the sieve; discard the seeds in the sieve. Set the saucepan aside. Add the strained grape puree to the grape skins in the blender and pulse a few times to coarsely chop the skins.

Transfer the entire mixture from the blender to the saucepan and bring to a simmer. Slowly add the remaining ¼ cup sugar, along with the pectin mixture, and stir until fully dissolved. Continue to cook until the jam has just thickened, about 3 minutes. Remove from the heat, transfer to a heatproof container, and let cool to room temperature. Cover and refrigerate the jam overnight to set.

NOTE: Jam can be stored in the refrigerator for up to 3 weeks.

McINTOSH APPLE BUTTER

Eating McIntosh apples from my grandfather's orchard in northern Wisconsin is a fond childhood memory. Before I could climb the trees and pluck them straight from the branches, I gathered them off the leaf-covered ground during autumn. With the apples too blemished to use for a pie or crisp, we'd cook up a batch of apple butter. Perfect on toast, as a garnish for a cheese plate, or even as a sundae topping, apple butter is a kitchen staple. MAKES 2 CUPS

3 large McIntosh apples

¾ cup packed dark brown sugar

½ cup apple cider

1 tablespoon dark spiced rum

Seeds from ½ vanilla bean

¼ teaspoon fine sea salt

¾ teaspoon ground cinnamon

Juice of ½ lemon

CORE THE APPLES and roughly chop into ½-inch pieces, keeping the skin on the fruit.

In a large saucepan, combine the apples, brown sugar, cider, rum, vanilla, salt, cinnamon, and lemon juice and bring to a boil. Reduce the heat to a simmer and cook until the liquid from the apples is released, stirring frequently. Continue to cook until almost all of the liquid has reduced, the apples have darkened in color, and they are completely soft, 20 to 30 minutes.

Using a slotted spoon, transfer the apples to a blender, reserving the excess liquid. Puree the apples until they are completely smooth, adding the cooking liquid sparingly as needed to blend, but taking care not to thin the consistency of the apple butter too much. Let cool to room temperature. Transfer to an airtight container and refrigerate until cold.

NOTE: Apple butter can be stored in the refrigerator for up to 2 weeks.

CHESTNUT-CHOCOLATE LAYER CAKE

This elegant cake will take center stage on a holiday table. The combination of ground chestnuts and chestnut flour used in the cake batter gives it a unique flavor and texture. Combined with caramel mousse filling, brown sugar buttercream icing, and a dark chocolate ganache glaze, it is a dessert to make for special occasions. Note that it takes advance planning and a large time commitment in the kitchen, but is worth the effort. MAKES 12 SERVINGS

Chestnut Cake

Nonstick cooking spray

8 ounces whole roasted chestnuts

1¾ cups cake flour

¼ cup plus 2 tablespoons chestnut flour

1½ teaspoons baking soda

¾ teaspoon fine sea salt

8 ounces (2 sticks) unsalted butter, softened

1 cup packed light brown sugar

½ cup granulated sugar

4 large eggs

¾ teaspoon pure vanilla extract

¾ cup sour cream

1 recipe Brown Sugar Buttercream (page 231)

1 recipe Caramel Mousse (recipe follows)

3 cups Dark Chocolate Ganache (page 229)

POSITION A RACK in the center of the oven and preheat to 350°F. Lightly coat three 8-inch round cake pans with nonstick cooking spray and line the bottoms of the pans with circles of parchment paper. Lightly coat the paper with nonstick cooking spray as well. Line a jelly-roll pan with parchment paper and place a wire rack on top. Grind the chestnuts, cake flour, chestnut flour, baking soda, and salt in a food processor until very finely ground.

In the bowl of stand mixer fitted with the paddle attachment, cream the butter, brown sugar, and granulated sugar on medium speed until light and fluffy. Add the eggs, one at a time, and the vanilla, and mix until evenly combined. Scrape down the sides of the bowl and add the ground chestnut mixture and the sour cream, alternating between the two, and mix until smooth.

Divide the batter evenly among the prepared cake pans and spread smooth. Bake until the cakes spring back to the touch and a knife inserted into the centers comes out clean, about 20 minutes. Let the cakes cool to room temperature in the pans. Carefully invert the pans to remove the cakes, and trim the tops of each cake to create three flat, even layers.

Fit a pastry bag with a ½-inch round pastry tip. Transfer about 1 cup of the buttercream to the prepared pastry bag. Set the remaining buttercream aside at room temperature until ready to use.

Place one cake layer on an 8-inch cardboard cake round. Pipe a ¾-inch-thick ring of buttercream on top of the layer, right at the edge of the cake. Fill the center of the ring of buttercream with half of the mousse and spread into an even layer, taking care to keep the filling inside the buttercream ring (fig. 1). Gently place a second layer of cake on top of

the mousse. Pipe another ring of buttercream around the edge of the layer and fill with the remaining mousse *(fig. 1)*. Place the remaining layer of cake on top of the mousse and freeze until the buttercream is fully chilled, about 1 hour.

Place the cake on top of a revolving cake stand and mound about three-quarters of the remaining buttercream onto the top of the cake. Using a large offset spatula, ice the top and sides of the cake with a thin and perfectly even layer of icing. Use the remaining buttercream to patch any holes or touch up any uneven areas, if necessary. Refrigerate the cake until the icing is set, about 30 minutes.

To glaze, set the cake on the wire rack–lined jelly-roll pan and slowly pour three-quarters of the ganache evenly over the top of the cake, allowing excess ganache to run down and coat the sides. Use the remaining ganache to coat any areas you may have missed. Let the ganache set for about 30 minutes before transferring the cake to a serving plate to slice.

NOTE: Reserve the extra ganache that pools up on the jelly-roll pan after coating the cake. When warmed again, it makes a great sauce to accompany each slice of cake.

Caramel Mousse

1 recipe Caramel Sauce
(page 228)

1 cup heavy cream

1 cup (8 ounces) mascarpone

IN THE BOWL of a stand mixer fitted with the whisk attachment, beat the caramel sauce, cream, and mascarpone until the mixture thickens and has a consistency similar to softly whipped cream. Lightly cover the mousse with plastic wrap and refrigerate until ready to use.

NOTE: I suggest breaking this recipe into two days of prep to avoid spending an entire day slaving away in the kitchen. Day One: Bake the cake and make the caramel sauce base for the mousse. Let the butter for the icing sit out overnight so it becomes incredibly soft. Day Two: Make the icing, finish the mousse, and assemble and ice the cake. Make the ganache last.

BANANA–BLACK WALNUT MUFFINS

Black walnuts have a distinctly different flavor from that of the more popular English walnut variety. I find most people either love or absolutely hate them. Give these nuts a chance. Yes, they are slightly pungent, but their earthy flavor, reminiscent of the exquisite black truffle, will grow on you, especially when they are folded into banana muffin batter and baked first thing in the morning. MAKES 12 MUFFINS

Nonstick cooking spray

2¼ cups unbleached all-purpose flour

½ teaspoon baking powder

1¼ teaspoons baking soda

3 to 4 ripe bananas, divided

1⅓ cups granulated sugar

½ teaspoon fine sea salt

⅔ cup canola oil

3 large eggs

⅔ cup (about 5 ounces) crème fraîche

1 cup (about 5 ounces) black walnuts, finely chopped

1 tablespoon turbinado sugar (optional)

POSITION A RACK in the center of the oven and preheat to 350°F. Lightly coat a 12-cup muffin pan with nonstick cooking spray or line with paper muffin liners. Sift the flour, baking powder, and baking soda together and set aside.

Puree 2 bananas in a blender or food processor to make a smooth banana puree. Slice the remaining bananas into twelve ½-inch-thick slices.

In a large mixing bowl, whisk the sugar, salt, oil, eggs, and crème fraîche together until smooth. Slowly add the dry ingredients and whisk until smooth. Stir in the banana puree and walnuts until evenly incorporated. Divide the batter evenly in the prepared muffin pan, filling each cup about three-quarters full. Gently press 1 banana slice into the top of each muffin, sprinkle generously with turbinado sugar (if using), and bake for 25 to 30 minutes, until golden brown and a knife inserted into the center of a muffin comes out clean.

BROWNED BUTTER WAFFLES

My waffles call for browned butter, giving their batter just an extra hint of toasty goodness. Since they are addictively delicious, my family begs for them each weekend morning, but I think they must be confused: I'm a pastry chef, not a short-order cook.

MAKES 5 OR 6 WAFFLES

2½ ounces (5 tablespoons) unsalted butter

1¾ cups unbleached all-purpose flour

1 tablespoon baking powder

½ teaspoon fine sea salt

3 tablespoons light brown sugar

1¾ cups whole milk

2 large eggs, separated

½ teaspoon pure vanilla extract

Nonstick cooking spray

IN A SMALL saucepan over low heat, melt the butter, stirring constantly, and cook until it is deep golden brown and smells toasted and nutty, about 4 minutes. Pour the butter into a heatproof bowl and set aside to cool to room temperature.

In a large bowl, whisk the flour, baking powder, salt, and brown sugar together until evenly combined. In another bowl, whisk the milk, egg yolks, vanilla, and browned butter together, then add to the dry ingredients. Whisk until completely smooth.

Preheat a waffle iron.

In the bowl of a stand mixer fitted with the whisk attachment, beat the egg whites on high speed for 2 to 3 minutes, or until thick, glossy, and tripled in volume. With a rubber spatula, gently fold the egg whites into the waffle batter.

Cook the waffles according to the waffle iron manufacturer's directions, lightly coating the iron with nonstick cooking spray before making each waffle. For one 7-inch waffle, you will use ¾ to 1 cup batter. Cook each waffle until very little steam escapes from the iron, 6 to 8 minutes each. Serve immediately.

(left) Browned Butter Waffles, *(right)* Banana–Black Walnut Muffins

JENNY'S MULLED APPLE CIDER

I enjoy making this recipe at the first sign of cold weather. The many spices give the cider a distinct, well-rounded flavor, which is more complex than most mulled drinks. As the pot comes to a boil and fills my kitchen with a fragrant aroma, it reminds me of the holidays just around the corner. MAKES 10 TO 12 SERVINGS

½ gallon fresh apple cider

4 cinnamon sticks

8 whole cardamom pods

12 whole cloves

Seeds and pod from
1 vanilla bean

Peel of ½ orange

½ teaspoon pink peppercorns

½ teaspoon black peppercorns

½ teaspoon whole
coriander seeds

12 whole allspice

8 whole star anise

¼ cup maple sugar

1 cup packed light
brown sugar

IN A LARGE pot, bring the cider, cinnamon, cardamom, cloves, vanilla seeds and pod, orange peel, pink peppercorns, black peppercorns, coriander, allspice, star anise, maple sugar, and brown sugar to a full boil. Remove from the heat and let the spices steep until the cider is just cool enough to drink. Divide among drinking glasses and serve immediately. Garnish with a few of the mulling spices from the pot.

NOTE: For a holiday party, try spiking the cider with dark rum or bourbon. But don't add the booze to the warm cider. Instead, keep the bottles alongside the simmering pot and let guests doctor their drinks if they desire.

HAZELNUT BRITTLE

During the mid-autumn hazelnut harvest, I like to use these nuts in recipes that let their flavor stand out. My brittle, requiring nothing more than a quick mix of salted caramel and toasted hazelnuts, is an easy way to make a satisfying version of this beloved American confection. MAKES ABOUT 16 PIECES

Nonstick cooking spray

2 cups (about 10 ounces) hazelnuts, skins on or off

2 ounces (½ stick) unsalted butter

1 cup granulated sugar

1 tablespoon honey

¼ cup water

¼ teaspoon fine sea salt

POSITION A RACK in the center of the oven and preheat to 350°F. Line a baking sheet with parchment paper and line a second baking sheet with a silicone baking mat. Lightly coat a heatproof spatula with nonstick cooking spray and set it on the silicone mat–lined tray.

Spread the hazelnuts on the parchment–lined baking sheet and bake until golden and fragrant, about 8 minutes.

In a medium saucepan, melt the butter over medium heat. Add the sugar, honey, water, and salt. Cook the caramel until it measures 365°F on a candy thermometer, gently swirling the caramel in the pan every few minutes. As soon as the caramel reaches temperature, immediately remove the pan from the heat, add the hazelnuts, and quickly stir once or twice to coat the nuts with the caramel. Pour the brittle onto the silicone baking mat–lined baking sheet and, using the greased spatula, spread the brittle into an even layer. Let it cool to room temperature, then break into small shards.

NOTES: Brittle can be stored in an airtight container for up to 2 weeks.

Make sure you never step away from cooking caramel, because in an instant the clear boiling solution will go from light brown to black. When the caramel reaches temperature, immediately remove it from the heat so it slows the cooking. Once nuts are added, the caramel will begin to harden, so be prepared to work quickly.

If you happen to burn the saucepan of caramel, don't use scrub pads to clean the pan. Fill the saucepan with water and let it simmer until the caramel dissolves.

(top left) Hazelnut Brittle, *(middle)* Coffee-Cardamom Shortbread, *(bottom right)* Autumn Chocolate Clusters

COFFEE-CARDAMOM SHORTBREAD

In the autumn, all of my favorite warm spices, especially cardamom, move to the front of the spice rack. Inspired by the traditional flavors of Turkish coffee, the addition of cardamom to these sandy cookies will have you hooked after one bite. MAKES ABOUT 36 COOKIES

12 ounces (3 sticks) unsalted butter, softened

½ cup confectioners' sugar

½ cup granulated sugar

3 cups unbleached all-purpose flour

¼ teaspoon fine sea salt

1 tablespoon finely ground coffee

2 teaspoons ground cardamom

POSITION TWO RACKS in the center of the oven and preheat to 350°F. Line two baking sheets with parchment paper.

In the bowl of a stand mixer fitted with the paddle attachment, cream the butter, confectioners' sugar, and granulated sugar until light and fluffy, about 3 minutes. Scrape down the sides of bowl. Add the flour, salt, coffee, and cardamom and mix until evenly combined, about 2 minutes.

Using a 1-ounce-sized ice-cream scoop, or a tablespoon, drop the cookie batter onto the prepared baking sheets about 2 inches apart. Gently press the cookies with flattened fingers and bake until light golden brown, 20 to 25 minutes. Let cool on the baking sheets to room temperature before serving.

NOTE: Shortbread is best eaten immediately, but can be stored in an airtight container for up to 5 days.

AUTUMN CHOCOLATE CLUSTERS

These satisfying clusters—a quick and easy confection to make throughout the fall—blend the flavors of toasted pumpkins seeds, cashews, and pecans with tart cranberries, rich dark chocolate, and a touch of sea salt. MAKES 30 CLUSTERS

½ cup (about 3 ounces) pumpkin seeds

1½ cups (about 7½ ounces) raw cashews

1 cup (about 4 ounces) pecan halves, roughly chopped

2 cups (about 12 ounces) dark chocolate chips

1 cup dried cranberries

¾ teaspoon coarse sea salt

POSITION A RACK in the center of the oven and preheat to 375°F. Line two baking sheets with parchment paper. Spread the pumpkin seeds, cashews, and pecans on one prepared baking sheet and bake until lightly toasted, about 5 minutes. Place the chocolate chips in a small, heatproof bowl.

Bring a small saucepan filled with about 1 inch of water to a simmer. Set the bowl of chocolate chips on top of the simmering water and melt, stirring occasionally. Remove from the heat and set aside.

In a large bowl, toss the cranberries, pumpkin seeds, cashews, and pecans together. Pour the melted chocolate over the mixture and gently stir to coat the fruit and nuts. Sprinkle with the salt and continue to mix until evenly combined.

With a tablespoon in each hand, scoop a heaping spoonful of the mixture into one tablespoon. Use the other tablespoon to push the mixture off the spoon and onto the prepared baking sheet, forming a little pile. Repeat with the remaining mixture. Refrigerate the clusters to set the chocolate before serving, about 30 minutes.

NOTE: Chocolate clusters can be stored in an airtight container in the refrigerator for up to 2 days.

CONCORD GRAPE AND ROSEMARY FOCACCIA

Tuscany's grape harvest is celebrated by bakers with a bread called *schiacciata con l'uva*. It's made with an olive oil focaccia dough, scattered with grapes and rosemary needles. My version is a little different because it calls for Concord grapes, a variety that is indigenous to the United States. The combination is wonderful, especially when served warm with a scoop of Vanilla Bean Ice Cream. MAKES 16 SERVINGS

½ cup extra virgin olive oil, divided

1½ teaspoons active dry yeast

1 cup water, warmed to about 110°F

1 teaspoon granulated sugar

2¾ cups unbleached all-purpose flour

2 teaspoons fine sea salt

¾ pound Concord grapes, stems removed

3 small sprigs fresh rosemary, stemmed

Coarse sea salt

1 recipe Vanilla Bean Ice Cream (page 232; optional)

POSITION A RACK in the center of the oven and preheat to 400°F. Lightly coat a 9 by 13-inch metal baking dish with 2 tablespoons of the oil.

In the bowl of a stand mixer fitted with the hook attachment, mix the yeast, water, 3 tablespoons of the oil, the sugar, flour, and fine sea salt on low speed until a ball forms, 3 to 4 minutes. Remove the bowl from the mixer, pour 1 tablespoon of the oil over the dough, and rub with the oil to completely coat. Cover the bowl with plastic wrap and set aside to rise until doubled in size, 30 to 45 minutes.

Cut the grapes in half and remove the seeds, keeping the skins with the grapes, if they come away from the fruit. Set aside until ready to use.

Transfer the risen dough to the prepared baking dish and evenly press the dough into the pan, covering the entire surface. Dock the dough with your fingertips, making holes all the way through. Drizzle the dough with the remaining 2 tablespoons oil. Sprinkle with rosemary needles, grapes and skins, and coarse sea salt. Lightly cover the pan with plastic wrap and set aside to rise until doubled in size, 20 to 30 minutes. Carefully remove the plastic wrap and bake until golden brown and a thermometer inserted into the center of the focaccia reads at least 200°F, 20 to 25 minutes.

Let the focaccia cool in the pan until warm. Slice and serve with ice cream (if using).

EARL GREY TEA–POACHED PEARS WITH FIGS AND POMEGRANATE

Some of my best recipes are a slight twist on a classic. For an updated version of poached pears, steep them in Earl Grey tea, which is rich with the fragrance of bergamot but light enough not to overpower such a delicate fruit. When served with fresh figs and pomegranates, they create an elegant and colorful dessert. MAKES 8 SERVINGS

4 cups water

2 cups granulated sugar

*Seeds and pod from
1 vanilla bean*

*8 Earl Grey tea bags,
tags removed*

Peel of ½ orange

¾ teaspoon fine sea salt

*8 ripe Forelle pears, or other
medium-sized variety*

16 ripe Black Mission figs

½ to ¾ cup pomegranate seeds

IN A LARGE covered pot, bring the water, sugar, vanilla seeds and pod, tea bags, orange peel, and salt to a boil. Remove from the heat and let steep for 15 minutes. Meanwhile, peel the pears.

Return the mixture to a full boil and, using a slotted spoon, place the pears in the poaching liquid. Reduce the heat to low, cover the pot, and let the pears gently simmer until they are fork tender, 15 to 20 minutes. Remove from the heat and let stand until the pears are cool enough to handle, 30 to 45 minutes. Using a slotted spoon, carefully transfer the pears to a shallow container. Strain the poaching liquid through a fine-mesh sieve over the pears, cover the container, and refrigerate overnight.

To serve, cut some of the pears and figs into halves, and the rest into quarters. Place the pears on a serving dish and garnish with figs and pomegranate seeds.

NOTE: Freeze any leftover poaching liquid for up to 6 weeks, for a future second batch, or discard.

BUTTERSCOTCH *BUDINO* WITH HOMEMADE CRÈME FRAÎCHE

During the cooler days of autumn, as gorgeous crimson, yellow, and orange leaves fall from the trees, I fall for warm, buttery flavors in my desserts. This **budino**, the Italian word for pudding or custard, is a little different because it calls for gelatin instead of the classic thickener, cornstarch. It makes a custard that is softer and smoother than most.

MAKES 10 SERVINGS

2 large eggs

1¾ teaspoons powdered gelatin

2 cups whole milk, divided

2 ounces (½ stick) unsalted butter

1 cup packed dark brown sugar

½ teaspoon fine sea salt

1 cup heavy cream

2 tablespoons Scotch

1 teaspoon pure vanilla extract

1 cup Homemade Crème Fraîche (page 230)

Chocolate shavings (optional)

PLACE TEN 4-OUNCE teacups or ramekins on a baking sheet. In a medium bowl, beat the eggs until smooth. In a small bowl, whisk the gelatin and ¼ cup of the milk together and set aside.

In a medium saucepan over medium-high heat, melt the butter. Add the brown sugar and salt, stirring until evenly combined and the mixture bubbles just around the edge of the pan. Add the cream, the remaining 1¾ cups milk, the Scotch, and vanilla and bring to a boil. Slowly pour the hot mixture over the eggs, whisking constantly. Add the gelatin mixture and whisk until combined. Strain the mixture through a fine-mesh sieve and divide evenly among the teacups. Refrigerate for 6 hours or overnight to set. Serve chilled, garnished with a large dollop of crème fraîche and a pinch of chocolate shavings (if using).

QUINCE-APPLE-PEAR CROSTATA

Rustic pies and tarts are delicious. Their homemade imperfections make them easy for the most inexperienced home bakers. For this crostata, do not worry about rolling the dough into a precise circle or arranging the fruit into a neat pattern. MAKES 10 TO 12 SERVINGS

3 ripe Comice pears

3 large Honeycrisp apples

3 medium quinces

½ cup granulated sugar, divided

Juice of ½ lemon

2 teaspoons grated fresh ginger

2 cinnamon sticks

2 tablespoons apple cider

Seeds from ½ vanilla bean

4 ounces (1 stick) unsalted butter, softened

½ cup packed light brown sugar

3 large eggs, divided

1 teaspoon brandy (optional)

½ teaspoon fine sea salt

½ teaspoon ground cinnamon

¼ cup plus 2 tablespoons unbleached all-purpose flour, plus more for dusting

½ recipe Perfect Pie Dough (page 225)

1 tablespoon turbinado sugar

POSITION A RACK in the center of the oven and preheat to 375°F. Line a baking sheet with parchment paper.

Peel, core, and cut the pears, apples, and quinces into ½- to ¾-inch slices. In a large bowl, toss the fruit with ¼ cup of the granulated sugar, the lemon juice, ginger, cinnamon sticks, cider, and vanilla until the fruit is evenly coated. Spread the mixture in a 9 by 13-inch glass baking dish and roast until the fruit is just tender, about 30 minutes. Transfer the baking dish to the refrigerator and let cool to room temperature. Remove the cinnamon sticks and discard.

In the bowl of a stand mixer fitted with the paddle attachment, cream the butter, brown sugar, and the remaining ¼ cup granulated sugar on medium speed until light and fluffy. Add 2 of the eggs and the brandy (if using) and continue to mix until evenly incorporated. Reduce the speed to low, then slowly add the salt, ground cinnamon, and flour, and mix until just combined. Set the filling aside until ready to use.

On a generously floured surface, roll the dough into an imperfectly shaped circle, 12 to 14 inches in diameter and ⅛ inch thick. Carefully roll the dough around the rolling pin, then unroll the dough onto the prepared baking sheet. Refrigerate until just firm, about 15 minutes.

Remove the chilled dough from the refrigerator and spread the filling evenly in the center of the circle, leaving about a 1½-inch border of dough uncovered. Scatter the roasted fruit evenly on top. Fold the edges of the dough over the fruit, pleating as needed. Beat the remaining egg by hand in a small bowl and lightly brush the entire surface of the folded dough edges with the beaten egg, taking care to brush between the pleats of dough. Firmly pinch the pleats of dough together to seal and prevent the filling from spilling out of the shell when baking. Sprinkle the entire crostata with turbinado sugar. Bake until the crust is deep golden brown and the edges of the fruit just begin to caramelize, about 45 minutes. Let cool on the baking sheet until just warm before slicing.

CONCORD GRAPE ICE POPS

My childhood summer days were spent with a purple-stained mouth and chin from grape-flavored ice pops. But as a seasonal pastry chef, I have switched this recipe to my fall repertoire when Concord grapes are ripe, making these chilled treats especially perfect for warm autumn evenings. MAKES EIGHT 3-OUNCE ICE POPS

1 pound Concord grapes, stems removed

2 cups water, divided

½ cup plus 2 tablespoons granulated sugar

Pinch of fine sea salt

IN A MEDIUM saucepan, bring the grapes and 1 cup of the water to a simmer and cook until the grapes soften and peel, about 10 minutes.

Transfer the mixture to a blender, add the remaining 1 cup water, the sugar, and salt, and puree until completely liquefied. Strain the mixture through a fine-mesh sieve into the bowl and divide evenly among ice-pop molds. Place 1 pop stick into each mold, submerging it about halfway, and freeze the pops overnight.

To remove the ice pops, let them stand at room temperature to soften for about 2 minutes, then firmly pull from the molds. If you have difficulty, run the molds under cool water to loosen, taking care not to get water on the pops, then firmly pull them from the molds.

PUMPKIN ROULADE

Pumpkin Roulade is the cake to make for a festive fall gathering. Everyone loves a rolled cake because it looks impressive. Reading this recipe through, you will realize that a roulade is not hard to make at all. The eggy batter gives this cake an ultra-moist and easy-to-roll texture, and the filling can be whipped up in just a few minutes. It can also be assembled a day or two in advance of serving. MAKES 10 TO 12 SERVINGS

Nonstick cooking spray

¾ cup unbleached all-purpose flour

¾ cup granulated sugar

¼ cup packed dark brown sugar

1 teaspoon baking soda

¼ teaspoon ground cinnamon

¼ teaspoon ground nutmeg

¼ teaspoon ground cloves

1 cup Roasted Sugar Pumpkin and Kabocha Squash (page 233)

3 large eggs

2 ounces (½ stick) unsalted butter, softened

1 cup (8 ounces) cream cheese, softened

¾ cup confectioners' sugar, plus more for dusting

Finely grated zest of ¼ orange

POSITION A RACK in the center of the oven and preheat to 350°F. Line a jelly-roll pan with parchment paper and lightly coat with nonstick cooking spray.

In a large bowl, whisk together the flour, granulated sugar, brown sugar, baking soda, cinnamon, nutmeg, and cloves until evenly combined. Add the roasted pumpkin and squash and the eggs and whisk until smooth. Using an offset spatula, evenly spread the batter into the prepared pan. Bake until the cake is set and springs back to the touch, 15 to 18 minutes. Let the cake cool to room temperature.

In the bowl of a stand mixer fitted with the paddle attachment, cream the butter, cream cheese, confectioners' sugar, and orange zest together until light and fluffy. Set the filling aside at room temperature until ready to use.

Remove the cake from the jelly-roll pan, keeping the parchment paper intact, and lay it on a flat work surface. Spread the filling in a thin, even layer over the entire surface of the cake. Starting at one of the wide edges of the cake, gently roll the cake into a tight log and peel away the parchment as you roll. Carefully transfer the roulade onto a serving platter, seam side down, and refrigerate until set, about 20 minutes. Dust generously with confectioners' sugar just before serving.

PERSIMMON PUDDING WITH GREEK YOGURT

James Tracey, the executive chef at Craft, always let me create my own desserts until the day he handed me a list of ingredients—no title, no instructions. With it came his request, "Can you please make this pudding for your fall menu? My mother-in-law, Lynda Scofield, gave me the recipe and it's my favorite." How could I have said no? To give it my own touch, I added a topping of Greek yogurt. MAKES 8 SERVINGS

Nonstick cooking spray

7 very ripe Fuyu persimmons, divided

¼ cup plus 2 tablespoons brandy

1 teaspoon pure vanilla extract

¾ cup whole milk, divided

2 large eggs

1¾ cups granulated sugar

2 cups unbleached all-purpose flour

4 teaspoons baking soda

2 teaspoons ground cinnamon

½ teaspoon fine sea salt

6 ounces (1½ sticks) unsalted butter, melted

1¾ cups (about 14 ounces) plain Greek yogurt

POSITION A RACK in the center of the oven and preheat to 325°F. Lightly coat eight 4 by 2-inch mini loaf pans with nonstick cooking spray. Place the prepared pans into a 9 by 13-inch baking dish.

Slice the tops from 4 persimmons and discard. Roughly chop the fruit and puree in a blender with the brandy, vanilla, and ½ cup of the milk until completely smooth. Transfer the puree to a large bowl and whisk in the eggs and sugar. Slowly whisk in the flour, baking soda, cinnamon, and salt. Add the remaining ¼ cup milk and whisk until smooth. Add the melted butter, whisking until no lumps remain in the batter.

Divide the batter among the prepared pans, filling them about three-quarters full, and tightly cover each pan with aluminum foil. Fill the baking dish with about ¾ inch warm water, cover the dish with another sheet of foil, and transfer it to the oven. Bake until the cakes have risen and spring back to the touch, about 1 hour and 15 minutes.

Remove the baking dish from the oven and carefully remove the foil from each pan. Let the cakes cool in the hot water bath until they reach room temperature. Run a butter knife around the edges of each cake to loosen and invert onto a serving platter. Lightly cover them with plastic wrap and refrigerate for 6 hours to overnight.

When ready to serve, slice the tops from the remaining 3 persimmons and cut the persimmons into ½-inch-thick slices. Stir the yogurt to soften and spread on top of the cakes. Decoratively arrange the persimmon slices on top of each cake.

Hachiya is an astringent variety of persimmon, and Fuyu is the most common nonastringent. Both have a distinct, yet delicate flavor of cinnamon and honeysuckle. Before eating, be sure that the persimmons are fully ripened. They should feel like a ripe tomato and give easily to gentle pressure.

CARAMEL LADY APPLES

A Halloween bash isn't complete without a good caramel apple. Having grown up on Chicago's north side, I enjoyed them freshly dipped and rolled in peanuts from Affy Tapple, the iconic maker of these kid-friendly costume-party treats.

MAKES ABOUT 20 APPLES

20 miniature Lady apples, or 12 medium, crisp apples

3 cups (about 12 ounces) roasted peanuts, finely chopped

2 cups granulated sugar

½ cup water

1 teaspoon fine sea salt

2 tablespoons light corn syrup

½ cup heavy cream

PIERCE THE TOPS of each Lady apple with a wooden ice-pop stick or candy dowel. Place the peanuts in a large bowl.

In a small saucepan, bring the sugar, water, salt, and corn syrup to a boil. Continue to cook over medium-high heat until the mixture reaches 370°F on an instant-read candy thermometer. Immediately remove from the heat and quickly stir in the cream, being mindful of steam. Let stand until the caramel thickens slightly, about 5 minutes.

Dip each apple into the caramel, taking care to cover the entire surface. Gently remove the excess caramel dripping from each apple by scraping the base of the apple on the edge of the pot. Place the dipped apple in the bowl of peanuts and roll to coat, using your hands to press the peanuts into the caramel, if necessary. Let the caramel set before serving, about 20 minutes. Caramel Lady Apples are best if eaten the same day.

NOTE: Be sure to cook the sugar solution for the caramel to 370°F. At that temperature, the mixture will be dark and may begin to smoke. Not to worry: Once the cream is added, the cooking process will immediately slow down, and the caramel will have an extra-rich flavor.

PUMPKIN–MILK CHOCOLATE PIE WITH A GINGERSNAP CRUST

The Thanksgiving table is never complete without a pumpkin pie. And for those bakers who are a little tired of the tried-and-true, give this recipe a shot. Its filling is classic, but the crust of ground gingersnaps and topping of milk chocolate ganache make for a much more flavorful slice than you may be accustomed to. MAKES 8 SERVINGS

Nonstick cooking spray

1½ cups (about 6 ounces) gingersnap cookie crumbs

2 tablespoons plus ½ cup packed light brown sugar, divided

¾ teaspoon fine sea salt, divided

2½ ounces (5 tablespoons) unsalted butter, melted

1½ cups Roasted Sugar Pumpkin and Kabocha Squash (page 233)

4 large eggs

1 large egg yolk

¾ cup heavy cream

1 tablespoon molasses

1 teaspoon pure vanilla extract

½ teaspoon ground cinnamon

¼ teaspoon ground ginger

¼ teaspoon ground nutmeg

1 recipe Milk Chocolate Ganache (page 229)

POSITION A RACK in the center of the oven and preheat to 350°F. Lightly coat a 9-inch pie plate with nonstick cooking spray.

For the gingersnap crust, stir together the cookie crumbs, 2 tablespoons of the brown sugar, ¼ teaspoon of the salt, and the butter until evenly combined and the mixture has the consistency of wet sand. Pour into the pie plate and, very evenly and firmly, pack the mixture into the base and up the sides of the pan, taking care to avoid too much buildup in the corner of the pan. Allow about ¼ inch of excess to rise above the top of the pan's edge.

Set the pie plate on a baking sheet and bake until the crust is slightly puffed and a bit darker in color, about 8 minutes. Let cool at room temperature for about 5 minutes, then transfer to the freezer until ready to use.

Reduce the oven temperature to 325°F.

In a large bowl, whisk together the remaining ½ cup brown sugar, the remaining ½ teaspoon salt, the roasted pumpkin and squash, the whole eggs, egg yolk, cream, molasses, vanilla, cinnamon, ginger, and nutmeg until completely smooth. Pour into the prepared piecrust and bake until the custard is set in the center when the pie plate is slightly jiggled, 50 to 60 minutes. Let cool to room temperature and refrigerate for 30 to 45 minutes to set.

Using the back of a spoon or ladle, spread the ganache in an even circle on top of the pie. Place the pie in the refrigerator until the ganache has just begun to set, 3 to 5 minutes. Remove the pie from the refrigerator and use the spoon or ladle to spread the ganache again to create a decorative, rustic texture. Refrigerate until fully set before slicing, about 20 minutes.

Oranger à fruits déprimés.

P. J. Redouté.   Langlois.

Milk Stout Cake with Malted Milk Buttercream
Panettone
Rose Water Truffles
Key Lime Meltaways
Bay Leaf Panna Cotta with Fresh Blood Orange
Meyer Lemon and Pistachio Tart
Pineapple Tarte Tatin
Passion Fruit-Buttermilk Sherbet
Banana Pudding Pops
Grapefruit-Aperol Sorbet
Meyer Lemon Italian Ice
Satsuma Chess Pie
Pecan Financiers

Winter

Iced Oatmeal Raisin Scones
Kumquat Marmalade
Chocolate–Dried Cherry Bread Pudding
Dirty Rice Pudding
Mardi Gras King Cake
Moonshine Eggnog
Grandma Charlotte's Rosettes
Toasted Coconut Biscotti
Holiday Hot Cocoa
Chocolate, Hazelnut, and Banana Trifle
Tropical Fruit Brown Betty
Coffee-Walnut Cake
Figgy Buckwheat Jam Bars

MILK STOUT CAKE WITH
MALTED MILK BUTTERCREAM

This unusual cake calls for milk stout, a heavy dark beer that is sweetened with lactose, the sugar derived from milk. The icing is made with barley malt syrup. I enjoy the rich flavor combination of the malt and beer, and the moist dense carrot cake–like texture, when the weather is bitter cold. MAKES 12 SERVINGS

Nonstick cooking spray

2½ cups unbleached all-purpose flour

1½ teaspoons baking soda

½ teaspoon fine sea salt

¾ teaspoon ground ginger

¾ teaspoon ground cinnamon

Pinch of cayenne pepper

8 ounces (2 sticks) unsalted butter, softened

¼ cup granulated sugar

¾ cup packed light brown sugar

2 tablespoons molasses

1 large egg

One 12-ounce bottle of milk stout beer, at room temperature

1 recipe Malted Milk Buttercream (page 231)

POSITION A RACK in the center of the oven and preheat to 350°F. Lightly coat two 8-inch round cake pans with nonstick cooking spray.

Sift the flour, baking soda, salt, ginger, cinnamon, and cayenne together into a bowl.

In the bowl of a stand mixer fitted with the paddle attachment, cream the butter, granulated sugar, and brown sugar together until light and fluffy. Add the molasses and egg and mix until smooth. Scrape down the sides of the bowl, reduce the mixer speed to low, and slowly add the dry ingredients and beer, alternating between the two, until the batter is fully combined. The batter may look curdled at this point, which is okay (see Note).

Divide the batter between the two prepared cake pans and bake until fully set, about 25 minutes. Let the cakes cool completely in the pans. Gently run a knife around the edge of the cakes and invert to remove them from the pans, rapping each pan lightly if needed to loosen.

Place one layer of the cake in the center of a serving plate. Top with about one-third of the buttercream and spread an even layer over the entire surface of the cake. Set the second layer of cake on top of the buttercream, taking care to center it perfectly on the first layer of cake.

Mound the remaining buttercream on the top of the cake and, using a large offset spatula, frost the top of the cake, while spreading the excess icing evenly onto the sides of the cake to create a thick layer of icing over the entire cake. Apply a bit of pressure to the tip of the spatula as you are icing to create a swirled texture. Serve immediately, or refrigerate until the icing is a bit set, about 30 minutes.

NOTE: The cake batter will look like it is curdling due to the large amount of liquid being added. Do not panic—when the sifted dry ingredients are combined in the batter, the texture will become smoother.

PANETTONE

Panettone, a traditional Italian sweet bread flavored with rum, raisins, and candied orange peel, is a customary Christmastime gift. Some recipes call for a slow proof time of around 20 hours to allow the bread to rise to its quintessential tall shape. My recipe takes time to make, but not that long. And, leftovers make incredible French toast. MAKES ONE 5-INCH ROUND LOAF

1 tablespoon plus
1½ teaspoons active dry yeast

¼ cup whole milk, warmed
to about 110°F

¼ cup honey

½ cup dark spiced rum

1½ cups raisins

Seeds of ½ vanilla bean

¾ teaspoon orange
blossom water

3 large eggs

1 large egg yolk

2½ cups unbleached
all-purpose flour, plus
more for dusting

2 teaspoons fine sea salt

4 ounces (1 stick) unsalted
butter, softened

½ cup candied orange
peel, chopped

Olive oil

¼ cup confectioners' sugar

IN THE BOWL of a stand mixer, gently stir the yeast, milk, and honey with a spoon, and set aside for a few minutes. In a small pot, bring the rum and raisins to a simmer over low heat. Remove from the heat, stir to coat the raisins in the rum, and transfer to a small bowl. Let cool to room temperature and set aside.

Fit the stand mixer with the hook attachment and add the vanilla, orange blossom water, eggs, egg yolk, flour, and salt to the bowl with the yeast mixture. Mix on low speed until the dough just comes together, 4 to 5 minutes. Add the butter, 1 tablespoon at a time, and continue to mix the dough for about 4 minutes.

Drain the excess rum from the raisins, reserving the rum, and add the raisins to the dough. Add the orange peel and continue to mix for about 3 minutes.

Turn the dough out onto a very generously floured surface, coat the entire surface of the dough in flour, and shape into a large ball. Carefully place in a 5¼ by 3¾-inch paper baking cup, gently brush the top with oil, cover loosely with plastic wrap, and set on two stacked baking sheets. Place in a warm area of the kitchen to rise until doubled in size, 50 to 60 minutes.

Position a rack in the center of the oven and preheat to 375°F.

Remove the plastic wrap from the dough and bake until the dough has a deep golden color, cover the top loosely with a piece of aluminum foil, and continue to bake until the center of the loaf reaches 200°F, about 60 minutes. Remove from the oven and let cool for 20 minutes.

In a small bowl, whisk the reserved rum and the confectioners' sugar together until smooth. Generously brush the glaze over the top of the loaf, continuing to glaze until all of it has soaked through. Let cool until just warm before serving.

ROSE WATER TRUFFLES

A charming box of hand-rolled truffles, flavored with a touch of rose water, is a delightful Valentine's Day gift. Be sure to use the finest quality chocolate available. It makes all the difference for this chocolate lover's indulgence. MAKES ABOUT 4 DOZEN TRUFFLES

½ cup (about 3 ounces) chopped semisweet chocolate

2 cups (about 12 ounces) chopped bittersweet chocolate, divided

1 cup heavy cream

1¼ teaspoons rose water

Pinch of fine sea salt

1 cup cocoa powder

2 cups (about 8 ounces) shelled pistachios, finely chopped

COMBINE THE SEMISWEET chocolate and 1 cup of the bittersweet chocolate in a large heatproof bowl.

In a small saucepan, bring the cream to a boil. Pour the cream over the chocolate mixture and let stand for 2 minutes to soften the chocolate. Add the rose water and salt and, using a rubber spatula, stir the mixture until the chocolate is fully melted and the mixture is perfectly smooth. Let the ganache cool to room temperature, then cover the surface directly with a sheet of plastic wrap and refrigerate overnight.

Line two baking sheets with parchment paper. Put the cocoa powder in a shallow bowl and the pistachios in another. Fill a small glass with very hot water.

Dip a ¾- to 1-inch round melon baller into the hot water, tap the excess water onto a paper towel, then scoop a round truffle from the firm ganache, taking care to create as round a truffle as possible. Knock the truffle from the melon baller onto one of the prepared baking sheets. Continue to scoop the truffles (dipping the melon baller into the hot water and tapping out the excess water each time), smoothing out the surface of the ganache as needed, until almost all of the ganache has been scooped. If the truffles are sticking to the melon baller, check to see if the water is still hot. If necessary, use your fingertip to push the truffles gently from the melon baller. Transfer the scooped truffles to the refrigerator to set, about 15 minutes.

In the top of a double boiler, melt the remaining 1 cup bittersweet chocolate over low heat. Remove the double boiler from the heat and let it sit at room temperature to keep the chocolate slightly warm.

Remove the truffles from the refrigerator and gently roll them between your palms to smooth any surface cracks or imperfections. If soft, return the truffles to the refrigerator to set before dipping, about 10 minutes.

Once the truffles are set, dip two or three fingertips into the melted chocolate *(fig. 1)*. Spread a generous amount of the melted chocolate on the palm of your other hand. Place one truffle in the center of your coated palm and, using dipped fingertips, roll until completely coated in melted chocolate *(fig. 2)*. Gently tilt your hand downward to let the coated truffle roll into either the bowl of cocoa or the bowl of pistachios *(fig. 3)*. Turn the truffle in the topping to completely coat. Transfer the coated truffle to the remaining prepared baking sheet and continue until all the truffles are coated. Refrigerate the truffles until set, about 15 minutes.

NOTES: For a thicker outer truffle shell, melt an additional 1 cup bittersweet chocolate and dip each truffle twice in the chocolate. Or skip coating the truffles in melted chocolate altogether. Instead, roll the balls of ganache directly in the cocoa powder or pistachios.

Truffles can be stored in an airtight container in the refrigerator for up to 1 week.

1   2   3

KEY LIME MELTAWAYS

The first pastry chef I worked under in Chicago, Celeste Zeccola, gave me this wonderful cookie recipe. During winter, when Florida's citrus is especially sweet, I spike her original vanilla version with Key lime juice. For light and delicate cookies, you need a stand mixer in order to whip enough air into the batter. MAKES 40 COOKIES

8 ounces (2 sticks) unsalted butter, softened

½ cup confectioners' sugar

4 teaspoons fresh Key lime juice

¼ teaspoon pure vanilla extract

Finely grated zest of ¼ lime

1¾ cups unbleached all-purpose flour

½ teaspoon fine sea salt

POSITION A RACK in the center of the oven and preheat to 350°F. Line a baking sheet with parchment paper. Fit a pastry bag with a ½-inch round pastry tip.

In the bowl of a stand mixer fitted with the paddle attachment, cream the butter, confectioners' sugar, lime juice, vanilla, and lime zest on medium speed until completely smooth, 1 to 2 minutes. Add the flour and salt and continue to mix on medium speed until light and fluffy, about 2 minutes.

Transfer the mixture to the prepared pastry bag and pipe small cookies in a swirl pattern onto the prepared baking sheet, about 1 tablespoon in size and about 1 inch apart. Bake until light golden brown, about 15 minutes. Let cool on the baking sheet to room temperature and serve.

NOTE: Meltaways are best eaten on the day they are made, but can be stored in an airtight container for up to 3 days.

BAY LEAF PANNA COTTA WITH FRESH BLOOD ORANGE

Chef Emeril's cuisine introduced me to the many uses of fresh bay leaves. Bay trees are abundant in New Orleans, and one grows in Emeril's backyard. While bay leaves are typically infused in stocks and sauces, I decided to steep them in this panna cotta recipe. The bay leaf adds a subtle minty flavor to the panna cotta—perfect topped with sweet blood orange segments. MAKES 8 TO 10 SERVINGS

½ cup plus 2 tablespoons granulated sugar

Pinch of fine sea salt

1 tablespoon plus 1 teaspoon powdered gelatin

3½ cups whole milk

1½ cups heavy cream

3 fresh bay leaves

Seeds of 1 vanilla bean

2 blood oranges

PLACE 8 TO 10 small glasses or ramekins on a baking sheet. In a small bowl, stir the sugar, salt, and gelatin together and set aside. Prepare a large bowl full of ice water and set aside.

In a medium saucepan, bring the milk, cream, bay leaves, and vanilla to a boil. Remove from the heat and let steep for 10 minutes. Return to a boil. Remove from the heat and, whisking constantly, slowly pour the gelatin mixture into the hot cream. Stir until fully dissolved. Pour the mixture into a large heatproof bowl, set it over the prepared bowl of ice water, and stir the panna cotta base until it is cooled to room temperature. Strain the mixture through a fine-mesh sieve into a spouted measuring cup or pitcher, discard the bay leaves, and divide the panna cotta base evenly among the small glasses. Loosely cover the glasses with a sheet of plastic wrap and carefully transfer to the refrigerator to set overnight.

Just before serving, peel and segment the blood oranges, taking care to remove all the pith, and reserve the juice. Garnish each panna cotta with a few slices of blood orange and a drizzle of the reserved juice.

(left) Key Lime Meltaways, *(right)* Bay Leaf Panna Cotta with Fresh Blood Orange

MEYER LEMON AND PISTACHIO TART

I adore Meyer lemons. During the fruit's peak season, I substitute Meyer lemon juice and zest in many recipes that call for common lemons. This pistachio-crusted tart, with its lemon-based curd filling, is sublime, especially for Meyer lemon fans like me.

MAKES ONE 14 BY 4½-INCH RECTANGULAR TART

½ cup (about 2 ounces) shelled pistachios

½ cup granulated sugar

4 ounces (1 stick) unsalted butter, softened

1 tablespoon pistachio nut paste

1 large egg

1½ cups unbleached all-purpose flour, plus more for dusting

Pinch of fine sea salt

1 recipe Meyer Lemon Curd (recipe follows)

Nonstick cooking spray

GRIND THE PISTACHIOS in a food processor into small pieces. Add the sugar and continue to grind to a powder.

In the bowl of a stand mixer fitted with the paddle attachment, cream the ground pistachios and butter on low speed until just combined. Add the pistachio paste and egg and continue to mix until evenly combined. Scrape down the sides of the bowl, add the flour and salt, and mix until the dough just comes together.

Turn the dough out onto a clean surface and gently knead until smooth. Press the dough into a flat disk, tightly wrap in plastic wrap, and refrigerate until firm, about 2 hours. Meanwhile, make the lemon curd.

Position a rack in the center of the oven and preheat to 375°F. Lightly coat a 14 by 4½-inch tart pan with a removable bottom with nonstick cooking spray.

On a lightly floured surface, roll the chilled dough into a large rectangle, about 17 by 6 inches. Use additional flour and give the dough a quarter turn between each roll to prevent it from sticking to the table. Continue rolling until the dough is an even ⅛ inch thick.

Carefully roll the dough around the rolling pin, then unroll it over the tart shell. Fit the dough into the pan by gently pressing it into the corners and against the base and sides of the pan, using the extra dough to patch any tears or holes. Freeze the lined tart pan, with excess dough hanging over the edge of the shell, to chill slightly, about 15 minutes.

Remove the tart pan from the freezer and trim away the excess dough from the edge of the shell using the back of a knife. Freeze the tart shell until frozen solid, about 15 minutes.

Line the tart shell with a sheet of parchment paper and fill it with pie weights or about 1 pound of dried beans. Place the tart shell on a baking

sheet and bake until the edges just begin to brown and the dough just sets, 12 to 14 minutes. Remove from the oven, carefully remove the weights or beans from the shell, and discard the parchment. Return the shell to the oven to continue baking for another 6 to 8 minutes, until the shell is fully baked. Let the shell cool to room temperature before filling. Reduce the oven temperature to 325°F.

Fill the tart shell with the lemon curd and gently spread smooth. Return the tart to the oven and bake until the filling slightly jiggles when tapped and is just set, about 15 minutes. Let cool completely before serving.

NOTE: Here are some things to keep in mind when making this dough: Due to the ground pistachios, it is fairly crumbly. If the dough tears when rolling or lining the tart shell, gently press it back together. There will be more dough than you will need to line the tart shell because the recipe calls for 1 whole egg. But do not discard the leftovers. Roll them into a ¼-inch-thick sheet, cut with a cookie cutter, and bake to make a delicious pistachio shortbread.

Meyer Lemon Curd

¾ cup plus 2 tablespoons granulated sugar

Finely grated zest of 4 Meyer lemons

1 cup fresh Meyer lemon juice

8 large egg yolks

3 large eggs

¼ teaspoon fine sea salt

8 ounces (2 sticks) unsalted butter, softened

BRING A MEDIUM pot filled with about 2 inches of water to a simmer. Prepare a large bowl of ice water and set aside.

In a large heatproof glass bowl, whisk the sugar, lemon zest, lemon juice, egg yolks, whole eggs, and salt together until evenly combined. Place the bowl over the simmering water and cook the mixture, whisking constantly, until it thickens and reaches 165°F, about 10 minutes.

Immediately remove the lemon curd from the heat, add the butter, and whisk until smooth. Place the bowl of curd over the prepared bowl of ice water. Stir until cooled to room temperature. Strain the mixture through a fine-mesh sieve into a bowl and refrigerate until ready to use.

NOTE: To save time, the Meyer lemon curd can be made in advance. Refrigerate for up to 3 days before filling and baking in the tart.

PINEAPPLE TARTE TATIN

Pineapple Tarte Tatin was one of the first recipes I learned to make in culinary school. Mastering the art of handmade puff pastry took a lot of practice. If you want to save time, use frozen puff pastry. It is a fine substitute as long as you buy a brand made with real butter. MAKES EIGHT 4-INCH TARTS

Nonstick cooking spray

1 large, ripe golden pineapple

2 sheets (14 ounces) frozen puff pastry, thawed

Unbleached all-purpose flour for dusting

4 ounces (1 stick) unsalted butter

¾ cup packed light brown sugar

½ teaspoon fine sea salt

¼ teaspoon ground black pepper

2 cinnamon sticks

4 whole star anise

Seeds of ½ vanilla bean

4 tablespoons brandy, divided

1 large egg, lightly beaten

1 recipe Passion Fruit–Buttermilk Sherbet (page 83; optional)

POSITION TWO RACKS in the center of the oven and preheat to 400°F. Lightly coat eight 4-inch cast-iron skillets with nonstick cooking spray and divide the skillets between two baking sheets.

Peel the pineapple and cut 8 slices crosswise, each about ½ inch thick, and remove the cores. If necessary, trim the rings to fit into the bottom of the skillets. Set the pineapple rings aside until ready to use.

Lay the sheets of puff pastry on a lightly floured surface. Using a fork, dock each sheet of dough, poking holes about ½ inch apart. Gently cut out eight 4½-inch rounds of dough and place them on a large platter. Transfer the rounds of cut dough to the freezer to chill, about 15 minutes.

In a large skillet, melt the butter over medium heat. Add the brown sugar, salt, pepper, cinnamon, star anise, and vanilla. Stir until the sugar is dissolved. Add 4 slices of pineapple and cook until just soft, 2 to 3 minutes on each side. Add 2 tablespoons of the brandy and cook the pineapple for 1 more minute. Reserving the juices in the pan, transfer 1 slice of the pineapple to each of four prepared cast-iron skillets. Repeat the cooking process with the remaining 4 slices of pineapple and the remaining 2 tablespoons brandy. Transfer the slices to the remaining four skillets, discard the cinnamon and star anise, and divide the remaining juices evenly among all of the skillets. Gently lift the slices of pineapple to allow the juices to seep underneath the fruit.

Remove the puff pastry rounds from the freezer and place 1 disk on top of each slice of pineapple. Using a butter knife, gently tuck the edge of the dough in between the pineapple and the pan. Lightly brush the disks of puff pastry with the beaten egg and bake until the puff pastry has risen and is deep golden brown, 30 to 35 minutes. Remove the tarts from the oven and let cool for 5 minutes. Carefully invert them onto serving plates. Top with a scoop of sherbet (if using).

PASSION FRUIT–BUTTERMILK SHERBET

On break from a particularly frigid Chicago winter, I vacationed in Buzios, a gorgeous Brazilian beach town. Every evening I marveled at the many dessert carts that lined the main street. Oversized glass cases, perched on mule-pulled carts or affixed to the front of bicycles, were filled with homemade custards, cakes, confections, and ice creams. My favorite dessert was a passion fruit sherbet made with sour milk. Upon my return home, I created this recipe reminiscent of my magical trip. MAKES 1 QUART

1 cup fresh or frozen passion fruit pulp, seeds removed

2 cups buttermilk

Juice of ½ lime

¼ cup light corn syrup

1 ½ cups granulated sugar

¼ teaspoon fine sea salt

IN A LARGE bowl, whisk the passion fruit pulp, buttermilk, lime juice, corn syrup, sugar, and salt together until the sugar is dissolved.

Freeze the mixture in an ice-cream machine according to the manufacturer's directions until the sherbet has a smooth, creamy texture. Store in the freezer for 4 hours before serving.

Light corn syrup is called for in several of my sherbet and sorbet recipes— ones that have a high water content. An invert sugar that inhibits crystallization, corn syrup helps create a creamy and smooth texture for frozen desserts. You can substitute a mild honey or light agave syrup for the corn syrup, but be aware that the flavor will vary.

(top left and bottom right) Pineapple Tarte Tatin,
(middle) Passion Fruit–Buttermilk Sherbet

BANANA PUDDING POPS

In the dead of winter, when I am tired of having little more than citrus to work with, I turn to the delicious banana, which is always in season. Made with fresh banana puree, sour cream, and store-bought Nilla Wafers, these pops are easy to make and satisfy my longing for summer. MAKES 10 TO 12 POPS

32 (about 4 ounces) Nilla Wafers

2 tablespoons plus ¼ cup packed light brown sugar, divided

2 pinches of fine sea salt, divided

2 ounces (½ stick) unsalted butter, melted

¼ cup granulated sugar

1⅓ cups whole milk

¼ cup sour cream

Seeds of ½ vanilla bean

3 ripe bananas

IN A FOOD processor, grind the Nilla Wafers into crumbs. Pour them into a large bowl, add 2 tablespoons of the brown sugar, 1 pinch of the salt, and the butter. Mix until combined and set aside.

Put the remaining ¼ cup brown sugar, the remaining pinch of salt, the granulated sugar, milk, sour cream, vanilla, and bananas in a blender and puree until completely smooth. Pour the mixture into a large bowl, add ½ cup of the Nilla Wafer mixture, and stir until just combined. Pour the base into ice-pop molds to ½ inch from the tops. Divide the remaining Nilla Wafer mixture among the tops of each of the ice pops, gently packing the molds.

Place 1 ice-pop stick in each mold, submerging it about halfway, and freeze overnight to set.

NOTE: If you have difficulty removing the pops when unmolding, run the molds under cool water to loosen, taking care not to get water on the pops.

GRAPEFRUIT-APEROL SORBET

Aperol is a brilliant orange Italian apéritif, which is made from bitter oranges, rhubarb, and a variety of herbs. I like Aperol best when it is mixed with freshly squeezed pink grapefruit juice to create this enticing cotton candy–colored sorbet. MAKES I QUART

4 cups fresh pink grapefruit juice

½ cup Aperol

½ cup light corn syrup

½ teaspoon fine sea salt

½ cup superfine sugar

IN A LARGE bowl, whisk the grapefruit juice, Aperol, corn syrup, salt, and superfine sugar together until the sugar has dissolved.

Freeze the mixture in an ice-cream machine according to the manufacturer's directions until the sorbet has a smooth, creamy texture. Store in the freezer for 4 hours before serving.

MEYER LEMON ITALIAN ICE

Meyer lemons were imported to the United States from China by the agricultural explorer Frank Meyer in 1908. A cross between a mandarin orange and a tart lemon, they are aromatic and much sweeter than common lemon varieties. I use them during their peak season, from November through March, especially for simple desserts like Italian ices, which highlight their unique flavor. MAKES 6 TO 8 SERVINGS

Finely grated zest of 4 Meyer lemons

2 cups fresh Meyer lemon juice

1 cup water

¾ cup light corn syrup

¾ cup superfine sugar

¼ teaspoon fine sea salt

COMBINE THE LEMON zest, lemon juice, water, corn syrup, superfine sugar, and salt in a large bowl and whisk until the sugar is completely dissolved. Strain the mixture through a fine-mesh sieve, then pour the mixture into a shallow dish. Freeze the mixture overnight, stirring every hour for the first 3 hours to help large ice crystals form.

Before serving, put 6 to 8 glasses in the freezer to chill, about 20 minutes. Scrape the ice with a fork, breaking up any large pieces that may remain in the bottom of the dish, then gently spoon the ice into glasses and serve immediately.

(left) Grapefruit-Aperol Sorbet, *(right)* Meyer Lemon Italian Ice

SATSUMA CHESS PIE

This recipe is an adaptation of my grandmother Ruth's chess pie, which calls for lemon juice. During winter, I substitute the grated zest of Satsuma tangerines for the lemon juice. The distinctive floral and pine-like flavor gives this classic southern pie's sugary custard filling a wonderful zing. MAKES ONE 9-INCH PIE

Nonstick cooking spray

½ recipe Blonde Sablé Dough (page 224)

1½ cups granulated sugar

2 tablespoons cornmeal

1 tablespoon unbleached all-purpose flour, plus more for dusting

¼ teaspoon fine sea salt

Finely grated zest of 2 Satsuma tangerines

½ teaspoon pure vanilla extract

⅓ cup whole milk

⅓ cup buttermilk

5 large eggs

2 large egg yolks

4 ounces (1 stick) unsalted butter, melted

POSITION A RACK in the center of the oven and preheat to 325°F. Lightly coat a 9-inch pie plate with nonstick cooking spray.

On a lightly floured surface, roll the dough into a circle about 12 inches in diameter by starting at the center of the disk and rolling away from you. Use additional flour and give the dough a quarter turn between each roll to prevent it from sticking to the table. Continue rolling until the dough is an even ⅛ inch thick.

Carefully roll the dough around the rolling pin, then unroll over the pie plate. Fit the dough into the pan by gently pressing it into the corners and against the base and sides of the pan. Trim the excess dough, leaving about a ½-inch overhang. Place the lined pan in the refrigerator until ready to bake.

In a large bowl, whisk the sugar, cornmeal, flour, salt, tangerine zest, vanilla, milk, buttermilk, whole eggs, egg yolks, and melted butter together until smooth. Pour the mixture into the prepared pie shell and bake until the custard has puffed and is set in the center, 45 to 50 minutes. If the crust takes on a deep golden brown before the filling has set, loosely tent a sheet of aluminum foil over the top of the pie to prevent the crust from burning and the custard from sticking to the foil.

Cool the pie on a wire rack to room temperature. Refrigerate the pie for about 2 hours to set before slicing and serving.

How this pie got its name remains uncertain. Some say early Americans mispronounced the word "cheese" when referring to the British classic lemon cheese pie. Others think the pie was named for its sugary filling, which allowed for storage in a pie chest instead of an icebox. But my favorite theory is that when a southern cook was asked what she was baking, her thick, drawled reply was "Jes pie."

PECAN FINANCIERS

Originally baked in Paris as an afternoon snack for the businessmen who worked in the stock exchange, these small cakes are named for their rectangular shape that resembles a bar of gold. I prefer the fancier traditional pointed oval shape. The browned butter in the batter makes financiers incredibly rich, perfect when paired with a cup of tea on a cold day. MAKES TWELVE 4-INCH FINANCIERS

Nonstick cooking spray

1 cup (about 4 ounces) pecans, divided

4 ounces (1 stick) unsalted butter

⅓ cup plus 2 tablespoons unbleached all-purpose flour

1 tablespoon honey

6 large egg whites

¾ cup granulated sugar

1 tablespoon turbinado sugar

POSITION A RACK in the center of the oven and preheat to 350°F. Lightly coat 12 financier molds with nonstick cooking spray and set them on a baking sheet. Fit a pastry bag with a round pastry tip.

Spread ¾ cup of the pecans on another baking sheet and toast until golden brown, about 8 minutes. Let the nuts cool to room temperature.

In a small saucepan over low heat, melt the butter, stirring constantly, and cook until it is deep golden brown and smells toasted and nutty, about 5 minutes. Pour the butter into a large heatproof bowl and set aside to cool to room temperature.

Grind the toasted pecans and flour in a food processor to a fine powder. Add the browned butter and honey and pulse until just combined. Transfer the mixture to a large bowl. Finely chop the remaining ¼ cup raw pecans by hand and set aside for topping.

In the bowl of a stand mixer fitted with the whisk attachment, beat the egg whites and granulated sugar on high speed until thick, glossy, and stiff, about 10 minutes. Gently fold the pecan mixture into the egg whites until smooth. Transfer the mixture to the prepared pastry bag and fill each financier mold almost full. Sprinkle the batter with the chopped pecans and turbinado sugar. Bake until light golden brown, about 20 minutes. Let the financiers cool in their molds until just warm enough to handle. Gently unmold onto a cooling rack.

NOTE: Financiers can be stored in an airtight container for up to 3 days.

ICED OATMEAL RAISIN SCONES

Inspired by classic iced oatmeal raisin cookies, these breakfast scones combine a little sweetness to start the day with such good-for-you ingredients as dried fruit and rolled oats. My recipe calls for the dough to be folded into thirds before rolling and cutting the scones. This technique creates light and flaky scones, which are especially nice when spread with Kumquat Marmalade (page 95). MAKES 16 LARGE SCONES

2 large eggs

1 cup heavy cream, divided

3 cups unbleached all-purpose flour, plus more for dusting

1 teaspoon ground cinnamon

1 tablespoon plus 2 teaspoons baking powder

¾ cup granulated sugar

½ teaspoon fine sea salt

6 ounces (1½ sticks) cold unsalted butter, cut into ½-inch cubes

⅓ cup Zante currants

½ cup golden raisins

½ cup old-fashioned rolled oats

2 tablespoons turbinado sugar, divided

½ recipe White Icing (page 231)

POSITION A RACK in the center of the oven and preheat to 350°F. Line two baking sheets with parchment paper.

Lightly whisk the eggs and ¾ cup of the cream together.

In a large bowl, whisk the flour, cinnamon, baking powder, granulated sugar, and salt together. Add the butter and gently toss by hand to coat in the flour mixture. Between your forefinger and thumb, press each cube of butter to flatten. Add the beaten eggs and cream and mix by hand until the dough just barely comes together and is very lumpy. Add the currants, raisins, and oats and gently knead into the dough.

Turn the dough out onto a generously floured surface and press into a large rectangle, about 1 inch thick *(fig. 1)*. Fold the dough into thirds, like a business letter (see page 94) *(fig. 2)*, adding flour to the top and underside of the dough as needed to prevent the dough from sticking to the table. Gently roll the dough into a large rectangle about ½ inch thick *(fig. 3)*.

Using a pizza wheel, cut the dough into triangles by cutting the dough into squares, then cutting them in half on a diagonal. Arrange the scones on the prepared baking sheets. Gather the scraps, gently roll out another rectangle of dough, and cut out additional scones. Lightly brush the tops of the scones with the remaining ¼ cup cream, sprinkle with 1 tablespoon of the turbinado sugar, and bake until golden brown, 25 to 30 minutes. Let cool on a rack to room temperature.

Drizzle the scones decoratively, or brush generously, with icing. Sprinkle the scones with the remaining 1 tablespoon turbinado sugar and let the glaze set for a few minutes before serving.

(left) Iced Oatmeal Raisin Scones, *(top right)* Kumquat Marmalade

NOTE: Scones are best served the day they are baked, but can be stored in an airtight container for up to 3 days.

Originally created in the early 1500s in Scotland, scones were once the triangle-shaped slices cut from large, round, and flat breads called bannock, which were made with unleavened oats and baked on a griddle. When baking powder became available, scones became leavened and baked in ovens instead, creating the lighter version of the bread we are familiar with today.

1   2   3

KUMQUAT MARMALADE

Mornings with my grandmother Ruth often begin with the British teatime snack of toasted crumpets spread with a dollop of homemade marmalade. This simple marmalade made with kumquats is my crowning contribution. MAKES 2 CUPS

1 pint kumquats

½ cup granulated sugar, divided

1 teaspoon powdered pectin

2½ cups water, divided

¼ teaspoon fine sea salt

SLICE THE KUMQUATS very thinly and remove and discard the seeds and stems. In a small bowl, stir 2 tablespoons of the sugar and the pectin together and set aside. Place a small plate in the freezer.

In a small saucepan, bring the kumquats and 1 cup of the water to a boil. Simmer for 1 minute, drain, and return the kumquats to the saucepan. Repeat with another 1 cup water. Add the remaining ½ cup water to the twice-drained kumquats, along with the remaining 6 tablespoons sugar and the salt, and bring to a simmer. Cook until the fruit is translucent and the liquid has reduced, about 5 minutes. Stir in the sugar and pectin mixture and continue to cook until thickened, 3 to 5 minutes.

Remove the plate from the freezer. Drop a small spoonful of jam onto the cold plate. If it sets to a soft jam consistency, remove the marmalade from the heat, transfer to a heatproof bowl, and let cool to room temperature. (If the marmalade is not quite set enough, continue to simmer for a couple more minutes and test on the cold plate again until it reaches the proper consistency.) Refrigerate overnight to fully set before serving.

NOTE: Marmalade can be stored in the refrigerator for up to 4 weeks.

Marmalade was first made from the Portuguese fruit marmelo (meaning "quince"). Eventually Seville oranges became the popular citrus ingredient for marmalade. What the two fruits have in common is high levels of pectin, making them perfect for preserving.

CHOCOLATE–DRIED CHERRY BREAD PUDDING

Rich, creamy, and slightly bound by bread, this dessert when served warm is perfect for a cold winter night. You may wonder how the soupy base will ever hold together, but once baked the pudding softly sets. Serve with a dessert spoon instead of a fork.
MAKES 8 SERVINGS

⅔ cup (about 4 ounces) dark chocolate chips

5 large eggs

¼ cup plus 1 tablespoon packed dark brown sugar

1 cup heavy cream

1 cup whole milk

2 tablespoons brandy

Finely grated zest of ¼ orange

Seeds of ½ vanilla bean

¼ teaspoon fine sea salt

¼ cup plus 1 tablespoon granulated sugar

6 slices soft white bread, cut into ½-inch cubes

½ cup (about 3 ounces) milk chocolate chips

½ cup dried cherries

Nonstick cooking spray

1 tablespoon turbinado sugar

PUT THE DARK chocolate chips in a large bowl. In another large bowl, whisk the eggs and brown sugar together until well combined.

In a medium saucepan, bring the cream, milk, brandy, orange zest, vanilla, salt, and granulated sugar to a boil. Pour the hot liquid over the dark chocolate chips and whisk until melted and smooth. Pour the dark chocolate mixture over the egg mixture, whisking constantly, and whisk until combined. Add the bread and gently stir to coat. Transfer the bread pudding mixture to the refrigerator to cool to room temperature. Stir in the milk chocolate chips and dried cherries. Cover and refrigerate overnight.

Position a rack in the center of the oven and preheat to 350°F. Place eight 4-ounce ramekins on a baking sheet and lightly coat the ramekins with nonstick cooking spray.

Stir the bread pudding mixture to evenly distribute the chocolate chips and cherries. Divide the mixture among the prepared ramekins. Sprinkle with turbinado sugar and bake until puffed and set, about 30 minutes. Serve warm or at room temperature.

DIRTY RICE PUDDING

Inspired by the classic New Orleans side dish, this popular dessert from my Emeril's restaurant repertoire calls for a laundry list of ingredients. Feel free to experiment by varying the spices, dried fruits, and nuts. MAKES 6 TO 8 SERVINGS

6 cups whole milk

¼ cup granulated sugar

2 tablespoons light
brown sugar

Seeds of 1 vanilla bean

1 fresh or dried bay leaf

¼ teaspoon ground cinnamon

¼ teaspoon ground cardamom

¼ teaspoon ground allspice

¼ teaspoon ground nutmeg

¾ teaspoon fine sea salt

Pinch of ground black pepper

¾ cup uncooked Arborio rice,
rinsed in cold water

¼ cup dried figs,
stems removed

¼ cup dried apricots

¼ cup raisins

Juice of 1 lime

Juice of 1 lemon

Juice of 1 orange

¼ cup (1 ¼ ounces)
whole natural almonds

¼ cup (1 ounce) shelled
pistachios

IN A 2-QUART saucepan, combine the milk, granulated sugar, brown sugar, vanilla, bay leaf, cinnamon, cardamom, allspice, nutmeg, salt, and pepper. Cover and simmer for 10 minutes. Remove the bay leaf and discard. Add the rice and cook, stirring often, until tender, 20 to 25 minutes. Remove from the heat and set aside.

Combine the figs, apricots, raisins, lime juice, lemon juice, orange juice, almonds, and pistachios in a food processor and pulse until coarsely chopped. Stir three-quarters of the mixture into the warm rice pudding. Garnish with the remaining chopped fruit and nut mixture just before serving.

NOTE: If you like rice pudding on the soupy side, warm an extra cup of milk and drizzle it evenly over each bowl of pudding.

MARDI GRAS KING CAKE

Like the floats that parade down St. Charles Avenue during Mardi Gras, this cake is grandiose. It wears a costume of icing and sparkling sugar and is meant to entertain. Traditionally, a little metal trinket in the shape of a baby is baked inside. As it goes in New Orleans, whoever gets the slice with the trinket is responsible for making next year's king cake. MAKES 16 TO 20 SERVINGS

1½ cups packed light brown sugar

1½ cups (about 5½ ounces) pecans, coarsely chopped

1½ teaspoons ground cinnamon

Finely grated zest of 1 orange

3 ounces (¾ stick) unsalted butter, softened

1½ recipes Honey Brioche Dough (page 223)

Unbleached all-purpose flour for dusting

1 large egg, lightly beaten

Nonstick cooking spray

1 recipe White Icing (page 231)

Silver dragées (optional)

Decorators' gold dust (optional)

Gold, green, and purple sugar (optional)

STACK TWO LARGE baking sheets on top of each other and line the top sheet with parchment paper. Place a wire rack over a third baking sheet and set aside.

Stir the brown sugar, pecans, cinnamon, orange zest, and butter together until evenly combined. Set the filling aside until ready to use.

Turn the dough out onto a lightly floured surface and press into a flat disk. Using a rolling pin, with very firm pressure, roll the dough into a large rectangle about ½ inch thick. Poke indentations in the dough with your fingertips to relax the gluten as you roll. This technique will also help prevent the rectangle from shrinking. Use additional flour and lift the sheet of dough as needed to keep it from sticking to the table.

Spread the pecan filling evenly over the entire surface of the dough and roll the dough into a tight log, starting with a long side. Carefully transfer the log, seam side down, to the prepared stack of baking sheets. Bring the two ends of the log together to form an oval, gently stretching the log as needed, to create a very large center hole. Lightly brush the ends of the log with the beaten egg, then seal by pressing the ends of the dough together very firmly. Cover the remaining egg with plastic wrap and set aside in the refrigerator. Lightly coat the dough with nonstick cooking spray, cover loosely with plastic wrap, and set aside to rise until about a third larger in volume, about 1½ hours.

Position a rack in the center of the oven and preheat to 450°F.

Gently brush the top and sides of the dough with the remaining beaten egg. Place the cake, on the stacked baking sheets, in the oven. Reduce the oven temperature to 350°F and bake until the cake is deep golden brown and the center reaches 200°F, 45 to 55 minutes. If the cake is dark in color, yet the center has not reached 200°F, cover the cake with

a sheet of aluminum foil to prevent further browning, and continue to bake until it reaches 200°F.

Remove the cake from the oven and let cool for about 20 minutes on the baking sheet. Carefully transfer the cake directly onto the prepared rack, discarding the parchment paper, and let cool to room temperature.

To finish the cake, slowly pour the icing over the entire cake, allowing it to drip over the sides. Sprinkle with silver dragées and gold dust (if using), or with the more traditional gold, green, and purple Mardi Gras–themed sugar (if using). Let the glaze set before slicing, about 10 minutes.

NOTES: If you want to hide a trinket in the cake, put it on top of the pecan filling before rolling the dough into a tight log.

If the surface of the cake cracks and some of the pecan filling finds its way onto the cookie sheet as it is baking, do not worry. Any imperfections will be hidden by the icing and decorations.

This recipe also makes exceptional cinnamon rolls. Instead of shaping the filled log into an oval, cut the log into 2-inch slices and arrange in a baking dish with about 1 inch of space in between each roll and the sides of the baking dish. Cover lightly with plastic wrap and let rise until nearly doubled in size. Remove the plastic and bake until the centers reach at least 200°F, about 25 minutes. If the rolls are a deep golden brown but the centers are less than 200°F, cover them with a sheet of foil and continue to bake until they reach the correct temperature.

MOONSHINE EGGNOG

This potent eggnog is a great holiday punch. Catdaddy Spiced Moonshine—made in a North Carolina distillery (and not at home in a bathtub)—has the smooth flavor of cinnamon, nutmeg, and vanilla, which mixes nicely with the rich cream and eggs.

MAKES 10 TO 12 SERVINGS

3 cups whole milk

1½ cups heavy cream

6 large eggs

¼ cup plus 2 tablespoons superfine sugar

¼ teaspoon fine sea salt

1½ teaspoons pure vanilla extract

Juice of ¼ lemon

¾ cup Catdaddy Spiced Moonshine

Ground nutmeg (optional)

IN A MEDIUM saucepan, bring the milk and cream to a boil. In a large bowl, whisk the eggs, superfine sugar, salt, and vanilla until smooth. Slowly pour the cream over the egg mixture, whisking constantly, until completely combined. Add the lemon juice.

Put the mixture in the refrigerator and let cool, stirring every so often, to about room temperature. Strain the mixture through a fine-mesh sieve into a bowl and refrigerate until chilled, 4 to 6 hours. Just before serving, add the moonshine and garnish each mug with a pinch of nutmeg (if using).

NOTE: In the summer months, this recipe makes a great Milk Punch, a classic New Orleans brunch cocktail. Omit the cream and eggs, and add crushed ice.

GRANDMA CHARLOTTE'S ROSETTES

Grandma Charlotte and I used to make these lovely rosette cookies together a few days before Christmas. The batter is simple enough for a child to whip up. However, frying is a bit trickier. Under the careful watch of Grandma, while teetering on a stool pulled to the stove top's edge, I was allowed to fry a few rosettes using her most prized kitchen utensil— her grandmother's antique rosette iron. MAKES 12 TO 15 ROSETTES

Canola oil for frying

1½ teaspoons granulated sugar

½ cup plus 2 tablespoons unbleached all-purpose flour

Pinch of fine sea salt

1 large egg

½ cup whole milk

½ teaspoon pure vanilla extract

Juice of ¼ lemon

Confectioners' sugar for dusting

OVER MEDIUM-HIGH HEAT, bring a large skillet filled with 2 to 2½ inches of oil to 375°F on a deep-frying thermometer. Line a large platter with paper towels.

In a small bowl, whisk the granulated sugar, flour, and salt together. Add the egg, milk, vanilla, and lemon juice and whisk until smooth.

Once the oil is at temperature, heat a rosette iron by dipping it in the oil for about 2 minutes. Blot the excess oil from the iron on a paper towel, dip the iron into the rosette batter, taking care to dip only about three-quarters deep, and then submerge the dipped iron into the oil to cook. Let the rosette fry in the oil until golden, 1 to 2 minutes, then gently push the rosette off the iron into the oil and continue to fry for another 20 to 30 seconds. Using chopsticks or a slotted spoon, transfer the rosette to the paper towel–lined platter to drain. Return the iron to the oil to reheat for a few seconds, and continue dipping and frying until little batter remains. Check the temperature of the oil after every few rosettes to make sure it remains at about 375°F. Increase the heat as needed. Let the rosettes cool to room temperature.

Generously dust with confectioners' sugar and serve immediately.

NOTES: The first few rosettes may stick to the iron and break when you remove them. Continue to dip the iron into the batter and fry. Eventually it will become seasoned and the rosettes will slip right off.

I recommend Nordic Ware's rosette iron (see Resource Guide, page 234). The company has been making exceptional Scandinavian baking tools in the United States for more than sixty years.

(left) Moonshine Eggnog. (right) Grandma Charlotte's Rosettes

TOASTED COCONUT BISCOTTI

The light and delicate texture of my biscotti is similar to shortbread. Refrain from snacking on the pieces as you slice them for toasting because they are more delicious after the second bake. MAKES 20 COOKIES

1 1/4 cups unsweetened coconut flakes

5 large egg yolks

1/2 cup plus 2 tablespoons granulated sugar

1/2 cup canola oil

1 teaspoon pure vanilla extract

Finely grated zest of 1/2 lemon

1 1/2 cups plus 2 tablespoons unbleached all-purpose flour, plus more for dusting

1/4 teaspoon fine sea salt

1 large egg, lightly beaten

POSITION A RACK in the center of the oven and preheat to 350°F. Line two baking sheets with parchment paper.

Spread the coconut on a baking sheet and toast until light golden brown, 5 to 7 minutes. Let the coconut cool completely before using.

In the bowl of a stand mixer fitted with the whisk attachment, beat the egg yolks and sugar on high speed until light, fluffy, and tripled in volume, about 5 minutes. Reduce the speed of the mixer, slowly add the oil and vanilla, and mix until evenly combined. Scrape down the sides of the bowl. Replace the whisk with the paddle attachment, add the lemon zest, flour, and salt, and mix on low speed until just combined. Scrape down the sides of the bowl, add the coconut, and continue to mix until evenly incorporated.

Turn the dough out onto a generously floured surface and gently roll into a log about 14 inches long. Carefully turn the ends of the log inward to make a ring, gently transfer to the prepared baking sheet, and reshape into a straight line. Using flattened fingers, gently press the top of the log to create a flat surface until it is about 1 inch thick and 3 inches wide. Lightly brush the entire surface of the biscotti with the beaten egg and bake until light golden brown and the dough springs back to the touch when pressed, about 25 minutes. Set the baking sheet on a rack to cool until the biscotti is warm enough to handle. Reduce the oven temperature to 300°F.

Transfer the biscotti to a large cutting board, reserving the parchment-lined baking sheet. Using a serrated knife, carefully slice the log into 1/2-inch pieces. Lay the slices flat on the baking sheet and return them to the oven to toast until very light golden brown, about 8 minutes. Gently turn the slices of biscotti over and toast for another 6 to 8 minutes. Let cool on wire racks to room temperature before serving.

(left) Holiday Hot Cocoa, *(right)* Toasted Coconut Biscotti

HOLIDAY HOT COCOA

Every year, I give spiced hot cocoa mixes to friends and family for the holidays.
By omitting the milk and cream from this recipe, you can make lovely year-end gifts.
Just bag the remaining ingredients, jot the recipe on a tag and tie it around the bag
with a festive ribbon. MAKES 6 SERVINGS

¼ cup cocoa powder

¾ cup granulated sugar

¼ teaspoon fine sea salt

½ cup (about 3 ounces)
milk chocolate chips

½ cup (about 3 ounces)
dark chocolate chips

1 cup heavy cream

3 cups whole milk

Seeds of ½ vanilla bean

2 cinnamon sticks

Finely grated zest of ½ orange

Ground cinnamon (optional)

IN A SMALL bowl, stir the cocoa, sugar, and salt together. Add the milk chocolate chips and dark chocolate chips.

In a medium saucepan, bring the cream, milk, vanilla, cinnamon sticks, and orange zest to a boil. Remove from the heat, add the cocoa mixture, and whisk until smooth. Let stand at room temperature to steep for about 5 minutes, stirring occasionally. Strain the hot cocoa through a fine-mesh sieve and serve immediately. Top with a dusting of ground cinnamon (if using).

CHOCOLATE, HAZELNUT, AND BANANA TRIFLE

Imagine stuffing a multilayered birthday cake into a bowl—that is my description of a trifle. Traditionally made with layers of custard, cake, nuts, and a splash of liquor, this version is scrumptious. MAKES ONE 8-INCH TRIFLE, OR 14 SERVINGS

For the super-dark chocolate cake layers:

Nonstick cooking spray

1⅓ cups unbleached all-purpose flour

¼ cup plus 3 tablespoons Dutch-processed cocoa powder

1 tablespoon instant espresso powder

¼ teaspoon fine sea salt

1 teaspoon baking soda

3 large eggs

1 teaspoon pure vanilla extract

1¼ cups granulated sugar

¾ cup canola oil

1 cup fresh brewed coffee, at room temperature

For the filling:

½ cup (about 2½ ounces) hazelnuts

4 cups heavy cream, divided

1 cup (about 6 ounces) semisweet chocolate chips

(ingredients continue)

MAKE THE SUPER-DARK chocolate cake layers: Position a rack in the center of the oven and preheat to 350°F. Lightly coat two 8-inch round cake pans with nonstick cooking spray.

Sift the flour, cocoa, espresso powder, salt, and baking soda together into a bowl and set aside.

In the bowl of a stand mixer fitted with the whisk attachment, beat the eggs, vanilla, and sugar on high speed until thickened and light in color, about 3 minutes. Gradually add the oil and continue to mix until evenly combined. Reduce the speed of the mixer to low, then gradually add the dry ingredients and coffee, alternating between the two until fully combined. Scrape down the sides of the bowl and mix until the batter is smooth.

Divide the batter evenly between the prepared pans and bake until a knife inserted into the center of the cake comes out clean, about 25 minutes. Leave the oven on. Let the cakes cool until they are cool enough to handle, then carefully invert the pans over a sheet of parchment paper and let cool to room temperature.

Meanwhile, make the filling: Spread the hazelnuts on a baking sheet and put in the oven to toast until the nuts are light golden brown and fragrant, about 8 minutes. Let cool to room temperature. Roughly chop them and set aside.

In a clean bowl of a stand mixer fitted with a clean whisk attachment, whip 1½ cups of the cream until soft peaks form. Transfer the cream to another bowl and set aside.

In the top of a double boiler, gently melt the chocolate chips. Remove from the heat, add the hazelnut butter, and stir until smooth.

¾ cup hazelnut butter

6 large egg yolks

¼ cup granulated sugar

¼ teaspoon fine sea salt

6 ripe bananas

To assemble:

½ cup Frangelico, divided

In a clean bowl of a stand mixer fitted with a clean whisk attachment, beat the egg yolks, sugar, and salt on high speed until lightened in color and tripled in volume, about 5 minutes. Remove the bowl from the mixer, add the chocolate and hazelnut mixture, and quickly fold together until evenly combined. Add the whipped cream and gently fold until smooth. Set the mousse aside in the refrigerator until ready to use.

In a clean bowl of a stand mixer fitted with a clean whisk attachment, whip the remaining 2½ cups cream to medium peaks and set aside. Peel and cut the bananas into ½-inch-thick slices.

To assemble the trifle, spread half of the mousse in the bottom of a trifle dish, cover with one-third of the whipped cream, sprinkle with about 2 tablespoons of the hazelnuts, and layer with one-third of the bananas. Firmly press one cake layer over the bananas and generously soak it with ¼ cup of the Frangelico. Repeat the steps to assemble a second layer. Top the trifle with the remaining whipped cream and decoratively arrange the remaining banana slices and chopped hazelnuts on top. Refrigerate until ready to serve.

NOTE: If you can't find hazelnut butter, Nutella will work just as well—but be sure to reduce the granulated sugar in the recipe to 3 tablespoons.

TROPICAL FRUIT BROWN BETTY

Brown Betty, a classic American comfort dessert, is traditionally cobbled together from day-old bread crumbs and leftover fruit. My recipe is an exotic update, substituting panko (Japanese bread crumbs) and coconut flakes for the bread—when baked, they make a light, crisp crust. MAKES TWO 7-INCH GRATIN DISHES OR ONE 8-INCH SQUARE PAN

2 ripe mangoes, peeled and pitted

½ ripe golden pineapple, peeled and cored

1½ cups panko bread crumbs

1½ cups unsweetened coconut flakes

6 tablespoons light brown sugar

¼ teaspoon fine sea salt

¼ teaspoon ground cinnamon

5 tablespoons unsalted butter, melted

Juice of ½ lemon

1 recipe Vanilla Bean Ice Cream (page 232; optional)

POSITION A RACK in the center of the oven and preheat to 350°F.

Cut the mangoes and pineapple into very thin slices and toss in a bowl to combine.

In a large bowl, mix the panko, coconut, brown sugar, salt, and cinnamon together. Slowly add the melted butter and stir until evenly combined. Divide half of the crumb mixture between the baking dishes (if using two dishes) and spread into an even layer. Cover with the slices of fruit. Drizzle the fruit with lemon juice and top with the remaining crumb mixture.

Cover the dishes with aluminum foil, place on a baking sheet, and bake for 20 minutes. Remove the foil and continue to bake until the topping is golden brown, 15 to 20 minutes. Serve warm with ice cream (if using).

The Tommy Atkins variety of mango, which was popularized by Florida growers in the 1950s due to its hardiness, is available during early winter in most grocery stores. Be sure the mango fully ripens before using, ensuring that it will have the sweetest flavor possible.

COFFEE-WALNUT CAKE

Walnuts, like coffee, have a slightly bitter taste, which comes from their skins. Combining these two ingredients with rich butter and mascarpone mellows this flavorful cake. I like to play up the walnut component by brushing each slice of warm cake with a touch of *nocello,* a wonderful walnut-based Italian cordial. MAKES ONE 9½-INCH CAKE

Nonstick cooking spray

1½ cups unbleached all-purpose flour

½ teaspoon ground cinnamon

¾ teaspoon baking powder

1¼ teaspoons instant espresso powder

Pinch of fine sea salt

5 ounces (1¼ sticks) unsalted butter, softened

¾ cup granulated sugar

3 large eggs

¼ cup (2 ounces) mascarpone

1⅓ cups (about 5½ ounces) walnuts, finely chopped

Nocello (optional)

1 recipe Whipped Mascarpone (page 230; optional)

POSITION A RACK in the center of the oven and preheat to 350°F. Lightly coat a 9½-inch savarin mold with nonstick cooking spray.

Sift the flour, cinnamon, baking powder, espresso powder, and salt together into a bowl and set aside.

In the bowl of a stand mixer fitted with the paddle attachment, cream the butter and sugar on medium speed until light and fluffy, 4 to 5 minutes. Add the eggs, one at a time, and continue to mix until smooth. Scrape down the sides of the bowl, reduce the speed of the mixer to low, add the plain mascarpone, and mix until just smooth. Slowly add the dry ingredients. Add the walnuts, increase the speed of the mixer to medium-high, and mix the batter for a few more minutes until smooth.

Spread the batter evenly into the prepared pan, place on a baking sheet, and bake until light golden brown, about 25 minutes. Remove the cake from the oven and lightly cover the pan with plastic wrap to collect steam as it cools until just warm.

To serve, gently invert the warm cake onto a serving platter, slice, brush lightly with *nocello* (if using), and garnish each slice with a dollop of whipped mascarpone (if using).

FIGGY BUCKWHEAT JAM BARS

While tinkering around with my fig jam bar recipe, I decided to add a little buckwheat flour to the dough. The result is fantastic, as the buckwheat gives the bars a hearty, unexpected flavor that befits a freezing cold day. MAKES 16 SMALL BARS

Nonstick cooking spray

1½ cups dried figs, stems removed, chopped

1⅓ cups dates, pitted and chopped

4 ounces (1 stick) unsalted butter, softened

½ cup plus 2 tablespoons packed light brown sugar, divided

1 large egg

1 teaspoon pure vanilla extract

1¼ cups unbleached all-purpose flour

½ cup buckwheat flour

1 teaspoon baking powder

½ teaspoon fine sea salt, divided

Finely grated zest of ½ orange

¼ cup plus 2 tablespoons water

1 tablespoon turbinado sugar

Confectioners' sugar for dusting (optional)

POSITION A RACK in the center of the oven and preheat to 375°F. Lightly coat an 8-inch square pan with nonstick cooking spray.

Place the figs and dates in the bowl of a food processor and set aside.

In the bowl of a stand mixer fitted with the paddle attachment, cream the butter and ½ cup of the brown sugar until smooth. Add the egg and vanilla and mix until evenly combined. Scrape down the sides of the bowl. Slowly add the all-purpose flour, buckwheat flour, baking powder, and ¼ teaspoon of the salt, and continue to mix the dough until well combined.

Divide the dough in half and press one half into a flat disk, wrap in plastic wrap, and refrigerate. Press the remaining half of the dough into the base of the prepared pan in a thin, even layer. Refrigerate the pan until the topping is prepared.

In a small saucepan, bring the remaining 2 tablespoons brown sugar, the remaining ¼ teaspoon salt, the orange zest, and water to a boil. Remove from the heat and pour the mixture over the dried fruit in the food processor. Process the mixture until it is a smooth paste. Spread the fruit mixture over the chilled dough in the pan in an even layer.

Remove the remaining dough from the refrigerator, unwrap, place between two sheets of parchment paper, and roll into an 8-inch square, trimming and patching pieces as needed. Remove the top layer of parchment and discard. Flip over the dough on the remaining sheet of parchment directly on top of the fruit mixture in the pan. Press the dough gently into place, and peel away the remaining parchment and discard. Sprinkle generously with turbinado sugar.

Bake the bars until light golden brown and the dough springs back to the touch, about 35 minutes. Transfer the pan to a rack to cool completely. Cut into bars and dust with confectioners' sugar (if using).

NOTE: Bars can be stored in an airtight container for up to 3 days.

21

Augusta Innes Withers, del.
1825.

Angel Food Cake with Elderflower-Blueberry Sauce

Beehive Baked Alaskas

Honey-Roasted Apricot Parfaits

Charlotte Russe with Apricot Jam

Cherry Jam Pie

Blueberry Buckle

Cherry Cola Sorbet

Blueberry–Almond Cream Tart

Chocolate Chip and Coconut Cupcakes with Lemony Cream Cheese Icing

Cocoa-Lavender Cream Puffs

Soufflé Crêpes with Vanilla-Scented Strawberries

Creole Cream Cheesecake with Warm Cherries

Triple Pistachio Pound Cakes

Good Morning Granola Bars

Sage Honey Madeleines

Orange Blossom and Pecan Baklava

Italian Pignoli Cookies

Strawberry-Mint Shortcakes

Strawberry- and Milk-Chocolate-Glazed Cake Doughnuts

Strawberry-Thyme Lemonade

Blueberry-Apricot Cobbler

Rhubarb Swirl Ice Cream

Rhubarb–Rose Water Crumble

Yogurt Panna Cotta with Hibiscus-Poached Rhubarb

Double Chocolate–Espresso Brownies

ANGEL FOOD CAKE WITH
ELDERFLOWER-BLUEBERRY SAUCE

Records of angel food cake recipes date from more than a hundred years ago. It is no wonder that this cake is one of the most beloved of American desserts. The airy, snow-white crumb is a gorgeous contrast to the deep golden-brown crust. When served alongside a fragrant sauce of elderflower cordial and blueberries, this cake is just heavenly. MAKES ONE 10-INCH TUBE CAKE

1 cup cake flour

½ teaspoon fine sea salt

1¼ cups superfine sugar, divided

12 large egg whites, at room temperature

1 teaspoon pure vanilla extract

1 teaspoon cream of tartar

1 pint blueberries

½ cup plus 1 tablespoon elderflower cordial, divided

¼ cup granulated sugar

¼ cup water

Finely grated zest of ½ lemon

½ cup confectioners' sugar, sifted

POSITION A RACK in the center of the oven and preheat to 400°F.

Sift the cake flour, salt, and ¾ cup of the superfine sugar twice into a bowl or onto a piece of parchment paper and set aside.

In the bowl of a stand mixer fitted with the whisk attachment, beat the egg whites, vanilla, and cream of tartar on medium speed until foamy, about 1 minute. Reduce the speed of the mixer, add the remaining ½ cup superfine sugar, increase the speed of the mixer to high, and beat until stiff but not dry peaks form. Remove the bowl from the mixer and gently fold in the sifted dry ingredients, in three or four additions, until just combined. Spoon the batter into an ungreased tube pan, spread the surface of the batter smooth, and gently tap the pan on the counter to remove any large air bubbles. Bake until golden brown, the cake springs back to the touch, and a knife inserted into the center of the cake comes out clean, 20 to 25 minutes. Remove the cake from the oven and set upside down on a rack to cool.

While the cake is baking, combine the blueberries, ½ cup of the elderflower cordial, the granulated sugar, water, and lemon zest in a medium saucepan and bring to a full boil. Reduce the heat and simmer for about 3 minutes. Remove the saucepan from the heat, add the confectioners' sugar and the remaining 1 tablespoon elderflower cordial, and stir until dissolved. Let cool to room temperature and set aside until ready to serve.

When the cake has cooled to room temperature, gently loosen it from the edge of the pan with a sharp knife and invert onto a serving platter. Serve each slice with a few spoonfuls of elderflower-blueberry sauce drizzled over the top.

BEEHIVE BAKED ALASKAS

I prefer an impressive dessert like baked Alaska to have the appearance of a masterpiece.
Rather than spread the meringue, which can look messy, I pipe the meringue to create
a distinctive hive shape. The addition of honey gives this dessert its darling name.

MAKES 9 SERVINGS

Nonstick cooking spray

*1 cup plus 1 tablespoon
cake flour*

¼ teaspoon fine sea salt

¼ teaspoon baking powder

¼ teaspoon baking soda

*2 ounces (½ stick) unsalted
butter, softened*

¼ cup (2 ounces) cream cheese

*½ cup plus 2 tablespoons
granulated sugar*

3 large eggs, separated

Finely grated zest of 1 lemon

Juice of ½ lemon

¼ teaspoon cream of tartar

*1 recipe Vanilla Bean Ice
Cream (page 232)*

*1 recipe Toasted Honey
Meringue (recipe follows)*

Honey for drizzling (optional)

POSITION A RACK in the center of the oven and preheat to 350°F.
Line a 9-inch square pan with parchment paper and lightly coat with
nonstick cooking spray.

Sift the cake flour, salt, baking powder, and baking soda into a bowl and
set aside.

In the bowl of a stand mixer fitted with the paddle attachment, cream
the butter, cream cheese, and sugar together until smooth. Scrape down
the sides of the bowl, add the egg yolks, lemon zest, and lemon juice,
and mix until just combined. Slowly add the dry ingredients and mix
until light and fluffy, 3 to 5 minutes. Transfer the batter to a large bowl
and set aside.

In a clean bowl of a stand mixer fitted with the whisk attachment, beat
the egg whites and cream of tartar on high speed until tripled in volume
and soft but not dry peaks form. Gently fold the whipped egg whites into
the batter in two additions, until just combined. Spread the batter in an
even layer in the prepared pan and bake until light golden brown and a
knife inserted into the cake comes out clean, 16 to 18 minutes. Let cool
to room temperature.

To assemble the baked Alaskas, cut nine 3-inch circles of the cake and
place each circle on a serving plate. Place a scoop of ice cream on top of
each cake circle. Quickly pipe a spiral of meringue over the cake and ice
cream, starting from the bottom and working your way up, taking care
to avoid gaps in the meringue as it is layered upward *(figs. 1–3).* Use a
kitchen torch to brown the meringue, then drizzle with honey (if using)
and serve immediately.

Toasted Honey Meringue

6 large egg whites

2 tablespoons plus 1 cup
granulated sugar, divided

½ cup water

1 cup honey

Pinch of fine sea salt

FIT A LARGE pastry bag with a ½-inch round piping tip.

In the bowl of a stand mixer fitted with the whisk attachment, mix the egg whites and 2 tablespoons of the sugar on low speed. Meanwhile, combine the remaining 1 cup sugar, the water, honey, and salt in a small saucepan and cook over medium heat until the mixture reaches 238°F on a candy thermometer. Remove from the heat, increase the speed of the mixer to medium-high, and very slowly pour the hot sugar mixture over the egg whites, taking care not to pour the mixture onto the moving whisk in order to prevent spraying. Increase the speed of the mixer to high and whisk until tripled in volume and the mixture becomes thick, glossy, and cooled to room temperature. Transfer the meringue to the prepared pastry bag and refrigerate until ready to use.

NOTE: This meringue may be prepared up to 3 days in advance. Store in the freezer and transfer to the refrigerator to thaw 2 hours before using.

There are three varieties of meringue—French, Swiss, and Italian. French is the easiest to make—it requires whipping egg whites into sugar. Swiss is a bit more involved, using the same technique as the French variety, but cooking the meringue in a bain-marie over simmering water. Italian, my favorite, is the most complicated. A boiling sugar syrup is slowly added to egg whites as they are whipped. It makes a thick and dense meringue that is stable at room temperature, in the refrigerator, or in the freezer.

1

2

3

HONEY-ROASTED APRICOT PARFAITS

For this delightful parfait, I pair amaretti cookies and apricots because they are made from the same ingredient—the tiny white seed found in the center of an apricot pit, called a kernel. Smash one open and see for yourself. The flavor of the seed is bitter, similar to almond extract, so taste only a very tiny sliver. MAKES 8 TO 10 SERVINGS

Nonstick cooking spray

12 ripe apricots

1 tablespoon honey

1 tablespoon light brown sugar

¼ teaspoon fine sea salt

2 cinnamon sticks, broken in half

32 small (about 4 ounces) amaretti cookies

1¼ cups heavy cream

1 recipe Apricot Sorbet (recipe follows)

POSITION A RACK in the center of the oven and preheat to 450°F. Line a jelly-roll pan with aluminum foil and lightly coat it with nonstick cooking spray. Pit and cut the apricots into quarters.

In a medium bowl, toss the apricots, honey, brown sugar, salt, and cinnamon together until well combined. Spread the fruit into a single layer on the prepared baking sheet and roast until the fruit just begins to brown on the edges, about 25 minutes. Let cool to room temperature, discard the cinnamon sticks, and refrigerate until ready to use.

Place the amaretti cookies in a zip-top plastic bag. Gently crush the cookies using the back of a wooden spoon, taking care not to completely pulverize. Place about ⅓ cup of the cookie crumbs in a small bowl, and set aside for the topping.

In the bowl of a stand mixer fitted with the whisk attachment, beat the cream to soft peaks. Refrigerate until ready to use.

In each of 8 to 10 small serving glasses, layer 2 teaspoons of amaretti cookie crumbs, a few heaping spoonfuls of apricot sorbet, a few slices of the roasted apricots, and a dollop of whipped cream. Repeat until the glasses are full or you run out of ingredients. Sprinkle the reserved cookie crumbs over the parfaits to garnish, and serve immediately.

NOTE: The best way to roast fruit is to set the oven at 450°F or higher. As the fruit cooks, you will smell the sugars burning. When removing the pan from the oven, the sugars will have blackened and may let off smoke—this is okay, as it adds rich flavor.

Apricot Sorbet

20 very ripe apricots

1 cup granulated sugar

Seeds and pod from
1/2 vanilla bean

1/4 teaspoon fine sea salt

3/4 cup water

3/4 cup white wine

PIT AND CUT the apricots in half. Prepare a large bowl of ice water and set aside.

In a large saucepan, bring the apricots, sugar, vanilla seeds and pod, salt, water, and wine to a full boil. Reduce the heat to medium and simmer until the fruit is soft and just beginning to break down, about 15 minutes. Remove from the heat, transfer the mixture to a heatproof bowl, and place over the bowl of ice water. Stir occasionally until cooled to room temperature.

Remove the vanilla bean pod and discard. Transfer the apricot mixture to a blender and puree until completely smooth. Strain the mixture through a fine-mesh sieve into a bowl and refrigerate the sorbet base overnight.

Freeze the sorbet base in an ice-cream machine according to the manufacturer's directions until the sorbet has a smooth, creamy texture. Store in the freezer for 4 hours before serving.

CHARLOTTE RUSSE WITH APRICOT JAM

I adore the McCoy family's Charlotte Russe more than any other dessert in this book. My grandfather Sandy, who taught me the virtues of cream sherry, made it especially for me for every holiday gathering. The combination of a rich mousse, sweet apricot jam, and crisp ladyfingers tastes as exquisite as it looks. This recipe has become a beloved family heirloom. MAKES ONE 8-INCH CHARLOTTE

2 tablespoons plus 1 cup granulated sugar, divided

3¼ teaspoons powdered gelatin

Pinch of fine sea salt

2 cups heavy cream

1 large egg

4 large egg yolks

¼ cup whole milk

3 tablespoons cream sherry

4½ to 5 dozen Italian savoiardi ladyfingers

1 recipe Apricot Jam (recipe follows; see note)

3 to 4 ripe apricots

IN A SMALL bowl, combine 2 tablespoons of the sugar, the gelatin, and salt and set aside.

In the bowl of a stand mixer fitted with the whisk attachment, beat the cream until stiff peaks form. Refrigerate until ready to use.

In a clean bowl of a stand mixer fitted with a clean whisk attachment, beat the whole egg, egg yolks, and the remaining 1 cup sugar until thick, glossy, and tripled in volume. Meanwhile, bring the milk to a simmer, add the gelatin mixture, and stir until fully dissolved. With the mixer running, slowly add the milk to the egg yolk mixture, then add the sherry and mix for about another 2 minutes, until evenly combined. Remove the bowl from the mixer and gently fold the whipped cream into the egg yolk mixture in two additions.

Line the interior perimeter of an 8-inch springform pan with ladyfingers, sugared sides out, standing upright. Tightly arrange a base layer of ladyfingers, sugared sides down, in the bottom of the pan to help hold the sides up. (This can be a little precarious—to make it easier, try lining the sides and the base simultaneously, allowing the base to help prop up the sides as you work your way around the pan.)

Spread half of the sherry mousse over the base of ladyfingers in an even layer. Spread the jam in an even layer over the mousse. Arrange another tight layer of ladyfingers on top of the jam and cover with the remaining mousse. Refrigerate for 3 to 4 hours to set.

Just before serving, pit and cut the apricots into ½-inch slices. Carefully remove the sides of the springform pan and garnish the top of the cake with the apricots. Tie a ribbon around the charlotte as a decorative finishing touch.

Apricot Jam

1 teaspoon plus ¾ cup
granulated sugar, divided

½ teaspoon powdered pectin

10 to 12 ripe apricots

¼ cup water

¼ teaspoon fine sea salt

IN A SMALL bowl, combine 1 teaspoon of the sugar and the pectin and set aside. Pit and roughly chop the apricots into ½-inch chunks.

In a medium saucepan, combine the apricots, the remaining ¾ cup sugar, the water, and salt and bring to a boil. Reduce the heat to low and simmer until the fruit breaks down and the liquid thickens, about 15 minutes. Slowly stir in the sugar and gelatin mixture until fully dissolved and cook for 3 more minutes.

Transfer the jam to a shallow, heatproof container and refrigerate, uncovered, until cold and set, about 1 hour.

NOTE: To shorten the prep time for this dessert, use store-bought apricot jam. Look for the best quality and thickest jam at the farmers' market first.

CHERRY JAM PIE

Making a lattice piecrust seems like a challenge at first, but if you give yourself plenty of time and follow each step precisely, you will create a blue-ribbon winner. As a reward for your perseverance, the cherry jam filling is really simple to make. MAKES ONE 9-INCH PIE

Nonstick cooking spray

Unbleached all-purpose flour for dusting

1 recipe Perfect Pie Dough (page 225)

2 pounds Bing cherries, pitted and cut in half

Finely grated zest of ½ lemon

¼ cup plus 2 tablespoons granulated sugar

¼ cup cornstarch

½ teaspoon fine sea salt

Seeds from ½ vanilla bean

½ cup cherry jam

1 large egg, lightly beaten

1 tablespoon turbinado sugar

POSITION A RACK in the center of the oven and preheat to 350°F. Lightly coat a 9-inch pie plate with nonstick cooking spray. Line a baking sheet with parchment paper.

On a lightly floured surface, roll one disk of dough into a circle about 12 inches in diameter by starting at the center of the disk and rolling away from you. Use additional flour and give the dough a quarter turn between each roll to prevent it from sticking to the table. Continue rolling until the dough is an even ⅛ inch thick. Repeat with the second disk of dough.

Carefully roll one circle of the dough around the rolling pin and unroll over the pie plate. Fit the dough into the plate by gently pressing it into the corners and against the base and sides of the plate. Trim the excess dough, leaving about a ½-inch overhang. Place the lined pie plate in the freezer for about 15 minutes to chill slightly. Roll the second piece of dough onto the rolling pin and unroll onto a sheet of parchment paper. Cut the dough into 1-inch-wide strips. Place the dough strips in the freezer to chill.

In a large bowl, stir the cherries, lemon zest, granulated sugar, cornstarch, salt, vanilla, and jam together until well combined.

Pour the cherry filling into the prepared pie shell and lay 4 strips of pie dough, evenly spaced, over the pie filling. Lay 3 more strips on a diagonal, weaving over and under the bottom strips to create a lattice pattern. Trim the excess dough from the strips to line up with the overhang of the shell. Fold the overhang in half, tucking the cut edge between the shell and the pie plate. Using your fingertips, decoratively crimp the edges together to seal. Place the pie in the freezer for 10 minutes to chill slightly.

Lightly brush the entire surface of the dough with the beaten egg and generously sprinkle with the turbinado sugar. Place the pie on the baking sheet and bake for 45 minutes. Reduce the oven temperature to 325°F and continue to bake for 30 to 45 more minutes, or until the crust is deep golden brown, the filling bubbles, and the liquid has just thickened. Cool on a wire rack until just warm before serving.

NOTES: Look for the best quality and thickest cherry jam you can find to give the pie a rich flavor. Check out the variety available at the farmers' market first.

To make the the lattice pie dough strips even more decorative, use a ruler to measure the strips perfectly. Cut them with a pastry or ravioli wheel to create a fluted edge.

Bing cherries were first cultivated in 1875 in Milwaukie, Oregon, by horticulturist Seth Lewelling and the foreman of his family orchards, Ah Bing. The following year, when the cherries exhibited at the Centennial Exposition in Philadelphia, people thought they were crab apples due to their surprisingly large size. Since then, they've become one of the most popular varieties of cherries across the United States.

BLUEBERRY BUCKLE

Some of the early versions of this old-fashioned American dessert would literally "buckle" due to the heavy fresh fruit filling. My delicious recipe sandwiches a dense layer of blueberries between a buttery crumb cake and crunchy streusel to ensure it will hold its shape. MAKES 9 TO 12 SERVINGS

Nonstick cooking spray

3 ounces (¾ stick) unsalted butter, softened

¾ cup granulated sugar

Finely grated zest of 1 lemon

¾ teaspoon pure vanilla extract

4 large eggs

¾ cup plus 2 tablespoons unbleached all-purpose flour

¼ teaspoon fine sea salt

1 pint blueberries

3 cups Streusel (page 228)

POSITION A RACK in the center of the oven and preheat to 325°F. Lightly coat an 8-inch square baking pan with nonstick cooking spray.

In the bowl of a stand mixer fitted with the paddle attachment, cream the butter, sugar, and lemon zest on medium speed until light and fluffy. Scrape down the sides of the bowl. Add the vanilla and the eggs, one at a time, and mix until smooth. Reduce the speed of the mixer to low, slowly add the flour and salt, and mix until just combined.

Pour the batter into the prepared pan and top with an even layer of blueberries, gently pressing the blueberries into the top of the batter. Cover with the streusel and bake until golden brown and a knife inserted into the center of the buckle comes out clean, 35 to 45 minutes. Serve warm or at room temperature.

CHERRY COLA SORBET

We all have junk food cravings—my weakness is cherry Coke. At a movie theater, I cannot sit for two hours without a 32-ounce ice-cold cherry Coke. To satisfy my taste addiction, I created a slushy sorbet by blending vanilla bean–poached Bing cherries with Coca-Cola.

MAKES I QUART

1 pound Bing cherries, pitted

¼ cup water

¼ cup plus 2 tablespoons granulated sugar

¼ teaspoon fine sea salt

Seeds from ½ vanilla bean

¼ cup plus 2 tablespoons light corn syrup

3 tablespoons Chambord (optional)

One 12-ounce can of Coca-Cola

PREPARE A LARGE bowl of ice water and set aside.

In a large saucepan, bring the cherries, water, sugar, salt, vanilla, corn syrup, and Chambord (if using) to a rolling boil. Reduce the heat to a simmer and cook until the cherries are soft and just beginning to break down, about 15 minutes. Remove from the heat, transfer the mixture to a heatproof bowl, and place over the prepared bowl of ice water. Stir occasionally until cooled to room temperature.

Transfer the mixture to a blender and puree until completely liquefied. Strain through a fine-mesh sieve into a bowl, then gently stir in the Coca-Cola, taking care not to create too much foam. Refrigerate the sorbet base overnight.

Freeze the mixture in an ice-cream machine according to the manufacturer's instructions until the sorbet has a smooth, creamy texture. Store in the freezer for 4 hours before serving.

BLUEBERRY-ALMOND CREAM TART

This tart is perfect for the almond lover because it uses almonds in four different ways. Its filling, a classic French frangipane made with whole almonds, almond paste, and almond extract, is combined with fresh blueberries. A topping of sliced almonds is the finishing touch. MAKES ONE 10-INCH TART

Nonstick cooking spray

Unbleached all-purpose flour for dusting

½ recipe Blonde Sablé Dough (page 224)

1 cup (about 5 ounces) whole almonds

½ cup plus 2 tablespoons granulated sugar

¼ teaspoon fine sea salt

¼ cup almond paste, roughly chopped

4 ounces (1 stick) unsalted butter, softened

2 large eggs

1 teaspoon pure almond extract

¾ pint blueberries

½ cup (about 2 ounces) sliced almonds

POSITION A RACK in the center of the oven and preheat to 350°F. Lightly coat a 10-inch tart pan with nonstick cooking spray and place it on a baking sheet lined with parchment paper.

On a lightly floured surface, roll the dough into a large circle by starting at the center of the disk and rolling away from you. Use additional flour and give the dough a quarter turn between each roll to prevent it from sticking to the table. Continue rolling until the dough is an even ⅛ inch thick.

Cut a large circle of dough, about 12 inches in diameter. Carefully roll the dough around the rolling pin, then unroll over the tart pan. Fit the dough into the pan by gently pressing it into the corners and against the base and sides of the pan, using the extra dough to patch any tears or holes. Trim away the excess dough from the edge of the pan with the back of a knife. Freeze the dough in the pan until fully hardened, about 15 minutes.

Bake the shell until light golden brown, 20 to 24 minutes. Rotate the baking sheet midway through the baking time and pierce gently with a fork if the center of the shell puffs up. Let cool to room temperature.

Grind the whole almonds until very fine in a food processor. Add the sugar, salt, almond paste, and butter and process until just combined. Scrape down the sides of the food processor, add the eggs and almond extract, and process until smooth.

Spread about 1 cup of the almond mixture into the prepared tart shell in an even layer. Scatter with the blueberries, then spread the remaining almond mixture over the top, filling the tart shell until just full. Sprinkle with the sliced almonds and bake until slightly puffed and golden brown, 40 to 45 minutes. Serve warm or at room temperature.

CHOCOLATE CHIP AND COCONUT CUPCAKES WITH LEMONY CREAM CHEESE ICING

I love to take a classic dessert and give it a simple twist to make it novel. For these cupcakes, which are based on my grandmother's coconut layer cake, I have varied the ingredients ever so slightly. I added chocolate chips to the angel food cake batter and lemon zest to the cream cheese icing. MAKES 12 CUPCAKES

1 cup unsweetened coconut flakes

½ cup cake flour

¼ teaspoon fine sea salt

½ cup plus 2 tablespoons superfine sugar, divided

6 large egg whites, at room temperature

½ teaspoon pure vanilla extract

½ teaspoon cream of tartar

¼ cup plus 2 tablespoons unsweetened shredded coconut

¼ cup (about 1½ ounces) semisweet chocolate chips, finely chopped

1 recipe Lemony Cream Cheese Icing (recipe follows)

POSITION A RACK in the center of the oven and preheat to 350°F.

Spread the coconut flakes on a baking sheet and bake until lightly toasted, 5 to 7 minutes. Let cool to room temperature and set aside until ready to decorate the cupcakes.

Increase the oven temperature to 400°F. Line a 12-cavity muffin pan with paper baking cups. Fit a pastry bag with a ½-inch round pastry tip.

Sift the cake flour, salt, and ¼ cup of the superfine sugar together and set aside.

In the bowl of a stand mixer fitted with the whisk attachment, beat the egg whites, vanilla, and cream of tartar on medium speed until foamy, about 1 minute. Reduce the speed of the mixer, add the remaining ¼ cup plus 2 tablespoons superfine sugar, then increase the speed of the mixer to high and beat until stiff but not dry peaks form. Remove the bowl from the mixer and gently fold in the sifted ingredients, the shredded coconut, and chocolate chips, in three or four additions.

Transfer the batter to the prepared pastry bag and pipe into the paper cups, filling them nearly full. Spread the surface of the batter smooth and gently tap the pan on the counter to remove any large air bubbles. Bake until golden brown, the cakes spring back to the touch, and a knife inserted into the center of a cake comes out clean, about 15 minutes. Let cool to room temperature.

Spread the icing over the tops of the cupcakes with a small spatula, or transfer the mixture to a pastry bag fitted with a desired pastry tip and pipe icing onto each cupcake.

Top with the toasted coconut flakes.

NOTE: Be sure to bake these cupcakes in paper baking cups. The cupcakes are delicate and a bit sticky, making removal from a muffin pan a challenge.

Lemony Cream Cheese Icing

3 ounces (¾ stick) unsalted butter, softened

1 cup (8 ounces) cream cheese, softened

½ teaspoon pure vanilla extract

Juice of ½ lemon

¾ cup confectioners' sugar

Pinch of fine sea salt

IN THE BOWL of a stand mixer fitted with the whisk attachment, beat the butter, cream cheese, vanilla, and lemon juice on medium speed until just smooth. Reduce the speed of the mixer, slowly add the confectioners' sugar and salt, and continue to mix until combined. Scrape down the sides of the bowl, increase the speed of the mixer to high, and beat the icing until light and fluffy, about 5 minutes.

COCOA-LAVENDER CREAM PUFFS

Lavender is a wonderful springtime ingredient. But when used in excess, it can cause a dessert to taste more like soap or perfume. For these cream puffs, I have combined a measured amount of fresh lavender with rich cocoa powder, milk, and bittersweet chocolate chips to balance the flavor of this very fragrant flowering herb.

MAKES 10 CREAM PUFFS

½ cup plus 2 tablespoons unbleached all-purpose flour

3 tablespoons cocoa powder

2 ounces (½ stick) unsalted butter

½ cup water

¼ teaspoon fine sea salt

2 tablespoons granulated sugar

3 large eggs, divided

1 tablespoon fresh lavender flowers (optional)

1 recipe Chocolate-Lavender Pastry Cream (recipe follows)

POSITION A RACK in the center of the oven and preheat to 350°F. Line a baking sheet with a silicone baking mat. Fit a pastry bag with a ½-inch round pastry tip.

Sift the flour and cocoa powder together and set aside.

In a small saucepan, bring the butter, water, salt, and sugar to a boil. Remove from the heat and slowly add the flour and cocoa mixture, stirring until a ball of dough forms and the dry ingredients are fully absorbed. Transfer the mixture to the bowl of a stand mixer fitted with the paddle attachment and mix on medium speed. Add 2 of the eggs, one at a time, and mix on medium-high speed until smooth and cooled to room temperature, about 5 minutes. Scrape down the sides of the bowl and the paddle frequently as the dough is mixing.

Transfer the dough to the prepared pastry bag and pipe it into large, round drops, about 2 inches wide and 1 inch high, a couple of inches apart. Beat the remaining 1 egg and lightly brush the tops and sides of the dough rounds. Sprinkle with a pinch of lavender flowers (if using) and bake until puffed, the surfaces are cracked, and the centers of the puffs are nearly baked all the way through, about 60 minutes. Let cool on a wire rack to room temperature.

Just before serving, slice the puffs in half lengthwise and pipe a few tablespoons of the chocolate-lavender pastry cream into the bottom half of each puff. Place the lid of each puff over the filling and eat immediately.

NOTE: Unfilled puffs will store for a couple of days in an airtight container, but their texture will soften. Before filling, pop them in the oven at 325°F for a few minutes to revive their crisp exterior.

Chocolate-Lavender Pastry Cream

⅔ cup whole milk

⅔ cup plus ½ cup heavy cream, divided

2 tablespoons fresh lavender flowers

3 large egg yolks

1 tablespoon cornstarch

¼ teaspoon fine sea salt

¼ cup granulated sugar

⅓ cup (about 2 ounces) milk chocolate chips

¼ cup (about 1½ ounces) bittersweet chocolate chips

IN A MEDIUM saucepan, bring the milk, ⅔ cup of the cream, and the lavender to a boil. Remove from the heat and let steep for 10 minutes. Return the mixture to a boil. Fit a pastry bag with a ½-inch star pastry tip.

In a medium bowl, whisk the egg yolks, cornstarch, salt, and sugar until completely smooth. Slowly pour the hot lavender cream over the egg mixture, whisking constantly. Return the mixture to the saucepan and cook over low heat, whisking constantly. Once the mixture starts to bubble, cook for another 1 to 2 minutes, until thickened, whisking constantly. Remove from the heat, add the milk chocolate chips and bittersweet chocolate chips and whisk until smooth. Strain through a fine-mesh sieve into a shallow container, cover the surface directly with plastic wrap, and refrigerate until cold and set, about 2 hours. Keep the remaining ½ cup cream in the refrigerator until needed.

Once cooled, transfer the pastry cream to a large bowl. In a separate bowl, whip the remaining ½ cup cream to stiff peaks, then gently fold it into the pastry cream until smooth. Transfer the cream into the prepared pastry bag and refrigerate until ready to use.

SOUFFLÉ CRÊPES WITH VANILLA-SCENTED STRAWBERRIES

These breakfast crêpes are a labor of love as they require constant attention at the stove top. Accompanied by Vanilla-Scented Strawberries, which can be prepared a day or two in advance, these cloudlike crêpes are best eaten immediately. MAKES 6 SERVINGS

6 large eggs, separated

2 cups whole milk

6 tablespoon plus 1 cup granulated sugar, divided

¾ teaspoon pure vanilla extract

3 ounces (¾ stick) unsalted butter, melted

1¼ cups unbleached all-purpose flour, sifted

Nonstick cooking spray

1 recipe Vanilla–Scented Strawberries (recipe follows)

IN A LARGE bowl, whisk the egg yolks, milk, 6 tablespoons of the sugar, the vanilla, melted butter, and flour together until smooth. Set aside. Evenly spread the remaining 1 cup sugar on a large plate.

In the bowl of a stand mixer fitted with the whisk attachment, beat the egg whites on high speed until stiff but not dry. Gently whisk the whipped egg whites into the crêpe batter until evenly incorporated, taking care not to deflate the whites too much.

Lightly coat an 8-inch nonstick frying pan with nonstick cooking spray and place over high heat until very warm. Reduce the heat to medium, pour one large ladleful of batter into the pan, and swirl around to evenly spread the batter in the base of the pan. Cook until the edges of the crêpe just begin to turn golden and, similar to a pancake, bubbles appear and the surface just begins to look matte. Using a small offset spatula, gently lift one edge of the crêpe and roll it in the pan toward you, sealing the crêpe closed by rolling back and forth in the pan for a few seconds *(fig.1)*. Gently roll each crêpe from the pan onto the sugar-covered plate and turn once to coat *(fig.2)*. Serve immediately with a spoonful of the strawberries.

NOTE: To cut down on the prep time, make the vanilla-scented strawberry sauce up to 3 days in advance and store in the refrigerator. You can also prepare the first part of the crêpe batter—egg yolks, milk, 6 tablespoons of the sugar, vanilla, melted butter, and flour—and refrigerate it in an airtight container for up to 2 days. When you are ready to serve the crêpes, take the batter mixture out of the refrigerator and bring to room temperature. Then proceed with the remaining recipe steps.

Vanilla-Scented Strawberries

1 pint strawberries, hulled
and cut into quarters

2 tablespoons
granulated sugar

Seeds from ½ vanilla bean

Pinch of fine sea salt

COMBINE THE STRAWBERRIES, sugar, vanilla, and salt in a sauté pan and simmer over medium heat until the fruit has broken down and the liquid has slightly thickened, 3 to 5 minutes. Serve warm or at room temperature.

CREOLE CREAM CHEESECAKE
WITH WARM CHERRIES

Louisiana has a tradition of calling foods grown or produced locally "Creole." For most, the word *Creole* conjures up images of crawfish, spicy jambalaya, and gumbo. Certainly, this cheesecake includes none of the above. Creole cream cheese—a tangy fresh cheese that is a cross between sour cream and traditional cream cheese—gives this cake a distinctive flavor. MAKES ONE 9-INCH CAKE

For the graham cracker crust:

Nonstick cooking spray

8 to 10 Homemade Graham Crackers (page 226)

2 tablespoons granulated sugar

2 tablespoons light brown sugar

¼ teaspoon fine sea salt

5 tablespoons unsalted butter, melted

For the batter:

4 cups (32 ounces) cream cheese, softened

Finely grated zest of 1 lemon

Seeds from 1 vanilla bean

1½ cups granulated sugar

5 large eggs

2½ cups (20 ounces) Creole cream cheese (or sour cream)

(ingredients continue)

MAKE THE GRAHAM cracker crust: Position a rack in the center of the oven and preheat to 350°F. Lightly coat a springform pan with nonstick cooking spray. Tightly wrap the outside of the pan with a sheet of plastic wrap to prevent water from seeping into the pan, followed by a sheet of aluminum foil. Grind the graham crackers into a fine powder in a food processor. Measure 1¼ cups graham cracker crumbs and set aside.

In a medium bowl, stir the 1¼ cups graham cracker crumbs, granulated sugar, brown sugar, and salt together. Slowly add the melted butter and stir until the mixture resembles wet sand. Transfer the mixture to the prepared pan and, using the flat base of a measuring cup, gently press into an even layer in the bottom of the pan.

Bake the crust for 12 to 14 minutes, or until golden brown and set. Let cool to room temperature, then place in the refrigerator until ready to fill.

Reduce the oven temperature to 325°F.

Make the batter: In the bowl of a stand mixer fitted with the paddle attachment, mix the cream cheese, lemon zest, and the vanilla on low speed until smooth, scraping down the sides of the bowl frequently. Slowly add the granulated sugar, increase the mixer speed to medium, and mix until light and fluffy. Stop the mixer and switch to the whisk attachment. On medium speed, add the eggs, one at a time, beating until smooth. Scrape down the sides of the bowl, add the Creole cream cheese, and mix until perfectly smooth.

For the cherries:

*1 ounce (¼ stick)
unsalted butter*

Seeds from ½ vanilla bean

*2 tablespoons light
brown sugar*

Pinch of fine sea salt

*1 pound Bing cherries,
pitted and cut in half*

POUR the cheesecake batter into the prepared crust and place the springform pan in a 9 by 13-inch baking dish. Fill the baking dish about halfway up the sides of the springform pan with hot water. Carefully transfer to the oven and bake until the cheesecake is slightly puffed, set in the center, and light golden brown, about 90 minutes.

Carefully remove the cheesecake from the hot water bath; let stand for about 30 minutes. Gently run a paring knife around the edge of the cheesecake to loosen it from the sides of the pan; let cool to room temperature. Remove the foil and plastic from the bottom of the pan, cover the top of the pan with a new sheet of plastic wrap, and refrigerate overnight.

Remove the sides of the springform pan.

For the cherries, in a large sauté pan, melt the butter over medium heat. Add the vanilla, brown sugar, salt, and cherries. Sauté the cherries until they just begin to soften and their juices thicken to a syrup, about 5 minutes. Just before serving, spoon the warm cherries over the entire cheesecake, or divide them among slices to garnish.

NOTE: If you do not have time to make homemade graham crackers, store-bought crackers or graham cracker crumbs will substitute nicely.

In a professional kitchen, it is common to use plastic wrap when baking. The heat of the oven will cause it to shrink and tightly fit around a pan. Do not worry—it will not come into contact with what you are baking.

TRIPLE PISTACHIO POUND CAKES

What makes this pale green pound cake distinctive is the several ways that the flavorful pistachio nut is used. It is ground into the flour for the batter. A pistachio nut paste is incorporated. And finally, it is coarsely chopped to form a crunchy topping.

MAKES 24 CAKES

Nonstick cooking spray

½ cup (about 2 ounces) shelled pistachios

6 ounces (1½ sticks) unsalted butter, softened

1 tablespoon almond paste, finely chopped

½ cup granulated sugar

3 large eggs

2 tablespoons pistachio nut paste

½ cup unbleached all-purpose flour

½ teaspoon baking powder

½ teaspoon fine sea salt

1 tablespoon turbinado sugar (optional)

POSITION A RACK in the center of the oven and preheat to 325°F. Lightly coat a 24-cavity mini muffin pan with nonstick cooking spray. Fit a large pastry bag with a ½-inch round pastry tip.

Grind the pistachios in a food processor to a fine powder and sift, reserving the larger pieces separately for later use; set aside.

In the bowl of a stand mixer fitted with the paddle attachment, cream the butter, almond paste, and granulated sugar until smooth. Add the eggs and pistachio nut paste, scrape down the sides of the bowl, and mix until smooth. Slowly add the flour, baking powder, salt, and sifted pistachio powder and mix until light and fluffy, about 3 minutes.

Transfer the batter to the prepared pastry bag and pipe it into the muffin molds, filling them about halfway full. Sprinkle the batter with the reserved ground pistachios and the turbinado sugar (if using). Bake until light golden brown and the cakes spring back to the touch, about 14 minutes. Let cool to just warm before serving.

(clockwise from top) Triple Pistachio Pound Cakes, Good Morning Granola Bars, Sage Honey Madeleines, Orange Blossom and Pecan Baklava, Italian Pignoli Cookies

GOOD MORNING GRANOLA BARS

This recipe was born from my obsession with keeping my pantry neat and tidy. During an annual spring cleaning, I decided to mix a batch of bars using a miscellany of grains, nuts, and dried fruit I had on hand. Much to my delight, the combination was successful, and is now a staple for mornings on the go. MAKES 16 BARS

Nonstick cooking spray

1 cup (about 5 ounces) hazelnuts, roughly chopped

3 cups old-fashioned rolled oats

4 cups puffed brown rice

¼ cup flaxseeds

¾ cup dried cherries, roughly chopped

¾ cup unsweetened coconut flakes, roughly chopped

¼ teaspoon fine sea salt

½ cup packed light brown sugar

½ cup honey

¼ cup olive oil

¼ cup canola oil

PLACE A RACK in the center of the oven and preheat to 350°F. Lightly coat a 9 by 13-inch baking dish with nonstick cooking spray. Spread the hazelnuts on a baking sheet and toast until light golden brown and fragrant, about 8 minutes. In a large bowl, toss the rolled oats, puffed rice, flaxseeds, cherries, coconut, and toasted hazelnuts to combine.

In small saucepan, combine the salt, brown sugar, honey, olive oil, and canola oil and simmer for 4 minutes. Slowly pour the warm mixture over the dry ingredients and stir until evenly coated. Transfer the entire mixture to the prepared pan and very firmly press into the pan while the mixture is still warm. (Be certain to apply a good amount of pressure, as any large air pockets will prevent the bars from holding their shape when cut.) Let cool to room temperature.

Using a ruler, measure and score lines to make 16 bars about 4½ inches in length and 1½ inches wide. Using a sharp knife or a pizza wheel, cut the bars following the scored lines.

NOTE: Granola bars can be stored in an airtight container for up to 1 week.

SAGE HONEY MADELEINES

During the first days of spring, I like to sweeten my desserts with aromatic varietals of honey. The delicate herbal flavor of sage honey adds complexity to these simple madeleines. MAKES ABOUT 30 COOKIES

Nonstick cooking spray

*1 cup unbleached
all-purpose flour*

½ cup cake flour

2 teaspoons baking powder

¼ teaspoon fine sea salt

*6 ounces (1½ sticks)
unsalted butter*

*12 fresh sage leaves, very
finely chopped, divided*

4 large eggs

½ cup granulated sugar

*3 tablespoons dark
brown sugar*

3 tablespoons sage honey

Finely grated zest of 2 lemons

POSITION A RACK in the center of the oven and preheat to 325°F. Lightly coat a madeleine pan with nonstick cooking spray. Fit a large pastry bag with a ½-inch round pastry tip.

Sift the all-purpose flour, cake flour, baking powder, and salt together into a bowl.

In a small saucepan over low heat, melt the butter and half of the sage leaves, stirring constantly, and cook until the butter is deep golden brown and smells toasted and nutty, about 5 minutes. Pour the butter into a heatproof bowl and set aside to cool to room temperature.

In the bowl of a stand mixer fitted with the whisk attachment, beat the eggs, granulated sugar, brown sugar, and honey on high speed until light and fluffy, about 5 minutes. Remove the bowl from the mixer and gently fold the dry ingredients into the egg mixture. Add the cooled butter, the remaining sage leaves, and the lemon zest and continue to fold together until just combined. Transfer the batter to the prepared pastry bag.

Pipe batter into the prepared molds, filling them about two-thirds full. Set aside the pastry bag until you are ready to prepare an additional batch. Bake until golden brown around the edges and the madeleines spring back to the touch, about 10 minutes. Remove from the oven and immediately turn the madeleines out of the pan onto a clean surface. Let cool to room temperature. Lightly coat the pan with more nonstick cooking spray and repeat the filling and baking with the remaining batter. Serve immediately, as madeleines are always best fresh from the oven.

NOTE: To prevent browning butter from becoming blackened butter, gently stir it frequently. This will keep the milk solids from sinking to the bottom of the pan and becoming scorched.

Sage honey is created by honeybees pollinating sage bushes. The nectar from the blossoms infuse the subtlest of sage flavor into their hive's harvest.

ORANGE BLOSSOM AND PECAN BAKLAVA

Crisp layers of toasted phyllo, filled with a rich paste made from dates and pecans, are soaked in orange blossom water and honey for a perfect treat to transition from wintertime to spring, when orange blossoms are in full bloom. MAKES 24 PIECES

Nonstick cooking spray

20 sheets (about 10 ounces) fresh or frozen phyllo dough, thawed

2 cups pitted dates

1½ cups (6 ounces) pecan pieces

3 teaspoons orange blossom water, divided

1 teaspoon pure vanilla extract

Finely grated zest of 2 oranges, divided

½ teaspoon fine sea salt

¼ teaspoon ground cinnamon

4 ounces (1 stick) unsalted butter, melted

1 cup orange blossom honey

POSITION A RACK in the center of the oven and preheat to 350°F. Lightly coat a 9 by 13-inch baking dish with nonstick cooking spray. Cover a large flat work surface with a sheet of parchment paper and place the stack of phyllo sheets on top. Cover the phyllo with a sheet of plastic wrap to prevent the dough from drying out.

Grind the dates, pecans, 2 teaspoons of the orange blossom water, the vanilla, the zest of 1 orange, the salt, and cinnamon in a food processor to make a coarse paste.

Place 1 sheet of the phyllo in the bottom of the prepared baking dish. Brush the entire surface of the phyllo very lightly with melted butter, starting from the center of the sheet and working outward to prevent tears, then layer with another sheet of phyllo, taking care to perfectly line up the corners of each layer. Repeat the layering process with 8 more sheets of phyllo to create 10 layers in the pan.

Spread the date paste over the phyllo in a thin, even layer, using your fingertips to gently push the paste around, and cover the entire surface. Repeat the phyllo and butter layering with the remaining 10 sheets of phyllo. Using a sharp knife, cut the unbaked baklava into 24 pieces in the pan.

In small saucepan, bring the honey, the remaining 1 teaspoon orange blossom water, and the remaining zest of 1 orange to a simmer. Slowly pour the honey mixture over the entire surface of the cut baklava, cover with aluminum foil, and bake for 30 minutes. Remove the foil and continue to bake until the phyllo is deep golden brown and crisp, about 10 minutes. Let cool to room temperature, then cut again along the original lines into 24 pieces.

NOTE: Phyllo dough is delicate and has the tendency to crack and tear, but not to worry: Once it's covered with honey and baked, the imperfections will disappear.

ITALIAN PIGNOLI COOKIES

My first visit to Italy was during the Easter holiday, when bakeries burst with festive confections, cakes, and cookies. My version of this Italian specialty, especially popular during Christmas and Easter, is a little different from the traditional recipe because it calls for orange zest—a marvelous addition to the rich flavor of toasted pignoli, Italian for pine nuts. MAKES ABOUT 36 COOKIES

2¾ cups (about 14 ounces) pine nuts, divided

1 teaspoon pure vanilla extract

1 large egg

¼ cup almond paste, roughly chopped

Finely grated zest of ½ orange

1 cup confectioners' sugar

½ cup unbleached all-purpose flour

¼ teaspoon baking powder

¼ teaspoon fine sea salt

POSITION A RACK in the center of the oven and preheat to 350°F. Line a baking sheet with parchment paper.

Place 2 cups of the pine nuts in a large, shallow bowl and set aside.

Combine the remaining ¾ cup pine nuts, the vanilla, egg, almond paste, and orange zest and grind in a food processor until smooth.

Transfer the processed mixture to the bowl of a stand mixer fitted with the paddle attachment, slowly add the confectioners' sugar, flour, baking powder, and salt, and mix until fully combined. Pinch off teaspoon-sized pieces of dough and roll between your palms into small balls. Drop the balls of dough into the bowl of pine nuts and roll to completely coat. If the nuts are not sticking to the dough, firmly press them into the cookie dough so they adhere. Place the cookies on the prepared baking sheet about 2 inches apart, gently press to flatten slightly, and bake until light golden brown, about 12 minutes. Serve warm or let cool on wire racks to room temperature.

NOTE: Pignoli cookies can be stored in an airtight container for up to 3 days.

STRAWBERRY-MINT SHORTCAKES

There are two opinions regarding America's classic springtime dessert, strawberry shortcake. Some like this dessert made with sponge or angel food cake. But I, having been raised in a southern family, prefer it made with buttermilk biscuits. My recipe's flaky buttermilk dough contrasts wonderfully with the creamy mascarpone filling and macerated berries. MAKES 12 TO 14 SERVINGS

¾ cup packed dark brown sugar, divided

3½ cups unbleached all-purpose flour, plus more for dusting

2 tablespoons baking powder

1¼ teaspoons fine sea salt, divided

5 ounces (1¼ sticks) cold unsalted butter, cut into ½-inch cubes

1 cup plus 3 tablespoons buttermilk, divided

4 pints strawberries, hulled and cut in half

¼ cup fresh mint leaves, julienned

¼ cup granulated sugar

2 cups Whipped Lemon Mascarpone (page 230)

POSITION A RACK in the center of the oven and preheat to 350°F. Line a baking sheet with parchment paper.

In a large bowl, whisk ½ cup of the brown sugar, the flour, baking powder, and 1 teaspoon of the salt together. Add the butter and gently toss to coat in the flour mixture. Between your forefinger and thumb, press each cube of butter to flatten. Add 1 cup of the buttermilk and mix with your hands until the dough just barely comes together and is very lumpy.

Turn the dough out onto a generously floured surface and roll into a large rectangle about 1 inch thick. Fold the dough into thirds, like a business letter (see page 92) *(fig. 2)*, adding flour to the top and underside of the dough as needed to prevent it from sticking to the table, then gently roll the dough into a large rectangle about ¾ inch thick.

Using a 3-inch round biscuit or cookie cutter, cut biscuits from the dough and arrange them on the prepared baking sheet. Gather the scraps and gently roll another rectangle of dough to cut additional biscuits. Lightly brush the tops of the biscuits with the remaining 3 tablespoons buttermilk and sprinkle generously with the remaining ¼ cup brown sugar. Bake until deep golden brown, 30 to 40 minutes. Let cool to room temperature.

Gently toss the remaining ¼ teaspoon salt, the strawberries, mint, and granulated sugar together and let stand for 10 to 15 minutes to macerate and release the juices from the strawberries.

To assemble the shortcakes, split the biscuits in half. Place the bottom halves on individual serving dishes and spoon some of the liquid from the strawberries over the shortcakes. Divide the mascarpone among the biscuits in large dollops, top with the strawberries, and cover each with a biscuit top. Let stand for a few minutes before serving.

STRAWBERRY- AND MILK-CHOCOLATE-GLAZED CAKE DOUGHNUTS

With their topping of fresh strawberry and milk chocolate glazes, my doughnuts are an indulgent morning treat. The preparation for these doughnuts requires far less effort than the fried variety because the batter is baked instead. MAKES 16 TO 18 DOUGHNUTS

Nonstick cooking spray

1 cup unbleached all-purpose flour

¼ cup plus 1 tablespoon cake flour

½ cup granulated sugar

¼ cup packed dark brown sugar

½ teaspoon baking soda

¼ teaspoon fine sea salt

⅔ cup canola oil

⅓ cup whole milk

3 tablespoons sour cream

1 large egg

Seeds from ½ vanilla bean

1 recipe Strawberry Glaze (recipe follows)

1 recipe Milk Chocolate Glaze (recipe follows)

Sprinkles (optional)

POSITION A RACK in the center of the oven and preheat to 350°F. Place a cooling rack over a parchment-lined baking sheet. Lightly coat a 6-cavity doughnut pan with nonstick cooking spray.

In a large bowl, whisk the all-purpose flour, cake flour, granulated sugar, brown sugar, baking soda, and salt together and set aside. In a small bowl, whisk the oil, milk, sour cream, egg, and vanilla until smooth. While whisking, slowly pour the liquid mixture into the flour mixture and mix until smooth.

Spoon the batter into the molds, filling them about two-thirds full. Set aside the remaining batter until you are ready to prepare an additional batch. Bake until light golden brown and the doughnuts spring back to the touch, about 10 minutes. Let cool in the pan for a few minutes, then turn the doughnuts out of the pan onto the rack to cool. Wipe away any excess crumbs from the pan, coat with nonstick cooking spray, fill with batter, and bake another round of doughnuts. Repeat until no batter remains.

Arrange the doughnuts neatly on the cooling rack, giving them about an inch of space between. Slowly pour or brush the strawberry or chocolate glaze over each of the doughnuts. Decorate with sprinkles (if using). Let stand for 10 to 15 minutes to allow the glazes to set before serving.

Strawberry Glaze

3 large, ripe strawberries, hulled and roughly chopped

1 cup confectioners' sugar, sifted

Pinch of fine sea salt

IN A SMALL bowl, mash the strawberries with the back of a fork until nearly liquefied. Slowly stir in the confectioners' sugar and salt until smooth.

Milk Chocolate Glaze

3 ounces (¾ stick)
unsalted butter

¼ cup whole milk

½ cup (about 3 ounces)
milk chocolate chips

¼ cup plus 2 tablespoons
confectioners' sugar, sifted

Pinch of fine sea salt

IN A SMALL saucepan, heat the butter and milk until the butter melts. Add the chocolate chips and cook over low heat, stirring constantly, until melted. Remove from the heat, slowly add the confectioners' sugar and salt, and whisk until smooth.

STRAWBERRY-THYME LEMONADE

The essence of spring is captured in my fresh lemonade recipe, a take on the old-fashioned American standard. It is a trio of satisfying sweet and savory ingredients—lemon, thyme, and strawberries. MAKES 8 TO 10 SERVINGS

2 pints strawberries, hulled
and roughly chopped

3 large sprigs of fresh thyme,
twiggy stems removed, plus
more for garnish if desired

Finely grated zest of 2 lemons

¾ cup fresh lemon juice

3 cups water

1 cup superfine sugar

PUREE THE STRAWBERRIES, thyme, lemon zest, lemon juice, water, and superfine sugar in a blender until liquefied. Strain the mixture through a fine-mesh sieve into a pitcher and refrigerate until cold. Serve the lemonade over ice. Garnish with a fresh sprig of thyme (if using).

(left) Blueberry-Apricot Cobbler, *(right)* Strawberry-Thyme Lemonade

BLUEBERRY-APRICOT COBBLER

There is a variety of different toppings one can use to make a cobbler—ranging from thickly sliced biscuits, drop biscuit batter, or crumble. My version calls for a light buttermilk drop biscuit batter made with almond paste and sprinkled with sliced almonds. It creates a crisp crust with pockets of soft dough to blanket the warm fruit filling. MAKES 12 SERVINGS

20 ripe apricots, pitted and thickly sliced

1 pint blueberries

¼ cup plus 3 tablespoons granulated sugar, divided

½ cup packed light brown sugar

2 tablespoons cornstarch

½ teaspoon fine sea salt, divided

Seeds from ½ vanilla bean

¼ cup almond flour

1 cup unbleached all-purpose flour

1 teaspoon baking powder

½ teaspoon baking soda

Finely grated zest of ½ lemon

3 tablespoons almond paste, roughly chopped

3 tablespoons cold unsalted butter, cut into small cubes

¾ cup buttermilk

¾ cup (about 3 ounces) sliced almonds

1 tablespoon turbinado sugar

POSITION A RACK in the center of the oven and preheat to 350°F. Place a 9 by 13-inch baking dish on a parchment- or aluminum foil–lined baking sheet.

In a large bowl, combine the apricots, blueberries, ¼ cup of the granulated sugar, the brown sugar, cornstarch, ¼ teaspoon of the salt, and the vanilla until evenly coated. Spread the mixture evenly in the baking dish and set aside.

In a large bowl, stir the remaining 3 tablespoons granulated sugar, the remaining ¼ teaspoon salt, the almond flour, all-purpose flour, baking powder, baking soda, lemon zest, almond paste, and butter together. Using your fingertips, gently press the pieces of almond paste and butter to soften. Slowly add the buttermilk and stir until the batter is just combined.

Dot the top of the fruit in the baking dish with heaping tablespoons of the batter. Sprinkle with the almonds and turbinado sugar. Bake until the topping is golden brown and the fruit begins to bubble, 35 to 45 minutes. Serve warm or at room temperature.

There are several theories about how this dessert got its name. Some report that the early settlers of America "cobbled" it together when they couldn't find ingredients to make more refined steamed puddings. Others say that, when baked, the cobbler resembles a cobblestone street.

RHUBARB SWIRL ICE CREAM

I am crazy about rhubarb and don't understand many people's aversion to such
a wondrous ingredient. This unique ice cream is a marvelous mixture of rich,
sweet cream and thick ribbons of tangy homemade rhubarb jam. MAKES I QUART

*1 pound trimmed
rhubarb stalks*

*1 tablespoon plus ½ cup
granulated sugar, divided*

1 teaspoon powdered pectin

Pinch of fine sea salt

Juice of ½ lime

*1 tablespoon grenadine
(optional)*

*1 recipe Sweet Cream Ice
Cream, softened (page 232)*

CUT THE RHUBARB stalks in half lengthwise, then cut into slices about
½ inch thick. In a small bowl, stir 1 tablespoon of the sugar and the
pectin together and set aside.

In a large saucepan, combine the rhubarb, the remaining ½ cup sugar,
and the salt and bring to a boil. Continue to cook until the mixture
thickens, skimming away any foam from the top of the liquid. After
about 10 minutes, slowly add the sugar and pectin mixture and stir until
fully dissolved. Reduce the heat to a simmer and cook for 2 minutes.
Transfer the jam to a shallow heatproof container, stir in the lime juice
and grenadine (if using), and let cool to room temperature. Cover and
refrigerate overnight.

To swirl the ice cream, layer large scoops of ice cream and heaping
spoonfuls of jam in a large container, pressing down gently to remove
any air pockets between the layers. Cover and freeze until firm before
serving, 2 to 4 hours.

NOTE: Jam can be stored in the refrigerator for up to 2 weeks.

RHUBARB–ROSE WATER CRUMBLE

When rhubarb makes its short annual appearance each spring, I incorporate it into desserts as much as I possibly can. One of my favorite ways to use fresh rhubarb is to bake it into a simple crumble. The addition of rose water in this filling accentuates the sweetness of the rhubarb's tart flavor. MAKES 10 SERVINGS

3½ pounds trimmed rhubarb stalks

1 cup plus 3 tablespoons granulated sugar

1 cup plus 3 tablespoons packed light brown sugar

½ teaspoon fine sea salt

Seeds from 1 vanilla bean

2 teaspoons rose water

Finely grated zest of 1 lime

2 tablespoons cornstarch

2½ cups Streusel (page 228)

1 recipe Rhubarb Swirl Ice Cream (page 165; optional)

CUT THE RHUBARB stalks into ¼-inch-thick slices and put them in a large bowl. Add the granulated sugar, brown sugar, salt, vanilla, rose water, and lime zest and toss to coat. Cover with plastic wrap and refrigerate overnight to macerate.

Position a rack in the center of the oven and preheat to 350°F. Line a baking sheet with parchment paper.

Drain the excess liquid from the rhubarb, reserving it for later use. Add the cornstarch to the rhubarb mixture and stir until evenly combined. Divide the filling among 10 ramekins, add 1 tablespoon of the reserved rhubarb liquid to each ramekin, and top with streusel, gently packing it down.

Place the ramekins on the prepared baking sheet and bake until the streusel is golden brown and the fruit filling begins to bubble over, 35 to 40 minutes. Let cool until just warm. Serve with ice cream (if using).

NOTE: The remaining rhubarb–rose water filling liquid makes a great homemade soda. Combine the strained juice with soda water to taste, and enjoy.

If you prefer your rhubarb desserts to be bright pink in color, look for the hothouse-grown variety of rhubarb, which tends to be available early in the season from the Pacific Northwest. And always purchase rhubarb that is firm and crisp, similar to a good bunch of celery.

Rhubarb Swirl Ice Cream, Rhubarb–Rose Water Crumble

YOGURT PANNA COTTA WITH HIBISCUS-POACHED RHUBARB

The contrasting colors of this elegant dessert, set in pretty parfait glasses, make for a dinner party knockout. The tangy flavor of the sheep's milk yogurt pairs perfectly with the tart rhubarb poached in aromatic hibiscus. MAKES 6 TO 8 SERVINGS

1¾ cups granulated sugar, divided

¼ teaspoon plus 1 pinch of fine sea salt

3¼ teaspoons powdered gelatin

¾ cup whole milk

¾ cup heavy cream

Seeds from ½ vanilla bean

2½ cups (20 ounces) sheep's milk yogurt

1 cup water

½ cup dried hibiscus (or 4 hibiscus tea bags, tags removed)

1 large trimmed stalk rhubarb

PLACE 6 TO 8 small glasses or ramekins on a baking sheet. Prepare a large bowl of ice water and set aside.

In a small bowl, stir ¾ cup of the sugar, ¼ teaspoon of the salt, and the gelatin together and set aside.

In a small saucepan, bring the milk, cream, and vanilla to a boil. Remove from the heat and, whisking constantly, slowly pour the gelatin mixture into the hot cream; stir until fully dissolved. Pour the mixture into a large bowl set over the bowl of ice water and stir the panna cotta base until cooled to room temperature. Discard the bowl of ice water, add the yogurt to the cooled panna cotta base, and stir until smooth. Strain the mixture through a fine-mesh sieve into a spouted measuring cup or pitcher, then divide evenly among the small glasses. Loosely cover the glasses with a sheet of plastic wrap and carefully transfer to the refrigerator to set overnight.

Bring the water, the remaining 1 cup sugar, the remaining pinch of salt, and the hibiscus to a boil. Reduce the heat and simmer until reduced by half, then set aside. Meanwhile, cut the rhubarb stalk in half lengthwise, cut into ¼-inch-thick slices, and put in a large bowl.

Strain the warm liquid through a fine-mesh sieve directly over the rhubarb. Cover with a sheet of plastic wrap placed directly on the surface of the liquid to keep the rhubarb submerged. Refrigerate until cold, about 3 hours. Reserve the poaching syrup to garnish the panna cotta.

Just before serving, garnish each panna cotta with 2 to 3 tablespoons of rhubarb and the poaching syrup.

DOUBLE CHOCOLATE–ESPRESSO BROWNIES

Every season deserves a great chocolate dessert. This recipe is a variation of my classic brownie recipe. The addition of espresso to the batter makes the brownies wonderfully addictive for coffee and chocolate lovers. MAKES 9 BROWNIES

Nonstick cooking spray

¼ cup cocoa powder

¼ teaspoon fine sea salt

¾ cup unbleached all-purpose flour

½ teaspoon baking powder

4 ounces (1 stick) unsalted butter

1 cup (about 6 ounces) semisweet chocolate chips

2 tablespoons instant espresso powder

1 cup granulated sugar

¼ cup packed light brown sugar

3 large eggs

¾ cup (about 4½ ounces) milk chocolate chips

POSITION A RACK in the center of the oven and preheat to 350°F. Lightly coat an 8-inch square pan with nonstick cooking spray. Sift the cocoa powder, salt, flour, and baking powder together into a bowl and set aside.

In a large heatproof bowl set over a pot of simmering water, stir the butter and semisweet chocolate chips together until melted. Remove from the heat, add the espresso powder, granulated sugar, brown sugar, and eggs, and whisk until smooth. Add the dry ingredients and gently fold until combined. Stir in the milk chocolate chips.

Spread the batter evenly into the prepared pan and bake for 30 to 35 minutes, or until the brownies have risen and the surface is slightly cracked. Let cool to room temperature in the pan. To ensure perfectly cut brownies, refrigerate them in the pan for 1 to 2 hours, or until quite firm. Cut the brownies using a sharp knife, then let them return to room temperature before serving.

The Red Magdalene Peach

Peppermint–Cacao Nib Ice Cream with Cocoa Pizzelle Cones
Peach and Sweet Corn Ice-Cream Cake
Pluot Preserves
Plum-Almond Torte
Ricotta Bavarian with Cantaloupe Soup
Vanilla Bean Semifreddo with Warm Blackberry-Lime Sauce
Cava-Chamomile Gelatin with Fresh Red Currants
Espresso Granita with Cocoa Cream
Chocolate–Peanut Butter S'mores
Nutella-Raspberry Crêpes
Blackberry Blintzes
Funnel Cakes

{ *Summer* }

Warm Peach Hand Pies
Prosecco Sabayon and Fresh Stone Fruit
Raspberry–Chocolate Chip Bundt Cake
Raspberry–Crème Fraîche Tarts
Raspberry-Lavender Floats
Red Currant Clafoutis
Nutty Meringues
Plum–Poppy Seed *Kolache*
Sicilian Spumoni Sandwiches
Market Berry Summer Pudding
Watermelon Ice with Lime Cream
White Peach and Huckleberry Crisp

PEPPERMINT–CACAO NIB ICE CREAM WITH COCOA PIZZELLE CONES

By substituting cacao nibs for the chocolate chips and steeping fresh peppermint in the ice-cream base, I've created a sophisticated take on my favorite ice-cream flavor, mint–chocolate chip. Once you have a scoop or two of this ice cream in a cocoa pizzelle cone, you will realize that making homemade ice cream and cones is well worth the effort. MAKES ABOUT 10 CONES

½ cup unbleached all-purpose flour

2 tablespoons cocoa powder

½ teaspoon baking powder

Pinch of fine sea salt

1 large egg

¼ cup plus 2 tablespoons granulated sugar

1 teaspoon pure vanilla extract

3 tablespoons unsalted butter, melted

1 recipe Peppermint–Cacao Nib Ice Cream (page 233)

SIFT THE FLOUR, cocoa, baking powder, and salt together into a bowl and set aside.

In a large bowl, whisk the egg and sugar together until smooth. Add the vanilla and butter and mix until smooth. Slowly add the dry ingredients and mix until completely smooth. Transfer the mixture to an airtight container and refrigerate overnight.

Preheat an electric pizzelle iron and bake heaping tablespoons of the batter, one cookie at a time, according to the manufacturer's directions. As each pizzelle is ready, remove the cookie from the iron with an offset spatula and, taking care not to burn your fingers, immediately shape it into a cone by wrapping it around a cream horn or ice-cream cone mold. Using a kitchen towel to protect your hand from the heat, hold the cone in place until it is firm and cooled, pinching any little surface cracks together with your fingertips while the cookie is still warm. Continue to bake and shape more cones with the remaining batter. Let the cones cool to room temperature. Just before serving, top each pizzelle cone with a large scoop of the ice cream.

NOTE: Pizzelle cones can be stored in an airtight container for up to 3 days.

PEACH AND SWEET CORN ICE-CREAM CAKE

This ice-cream layer cake is rich with southern components: a corn bread–like cake, a sherbet of fresh peaches and tangy buttermilk, and sweet corn ice cream. Kentucky bourbon would make a mighty fine accompaniment. MAKES ONE 8-INCH ROUND CAKE

Nonstick cooking spray

½ cup plus 1 tablespoon unbleached all-purpose flour

½ cup stone-ground cornmeal

1 teaspoon baking powder

½ teaspoon fine sea salt

2 large, ripe peaches, divided

2 ounces (½ stick) unsalted butter, softened

½ cup granulated sugar

1 large egg

1 teaspoon pure vanilla extract

½ cup whole milk

1 recipe Sweet Corn Ice Cream, softened (recipe follows)

1 recipe Peach-Buttermilk Sherbet (recipe follows)

¾ cup heavy cream

POSITION A RACK in the center of the oven and preheat to 350°F. Line an 8-inch round cake pan with parchment paper and lightly coat with nonstick cooking spray.

In a small bowl, stir the flour, cornmeal, baking powder, and salt together. Pit and chop 1 peach into ½-inch chunks, keeping the skin on the fruit.

In the bowl of a stand mixer fitted with the paddle attachment, cream the butter and sugar until light and fluffy. Add the egg and vanilla and continue to mix until combined. Scrape down the sides of the bowl, slowly add the dry ingredients and milk, alternating between the two, and mix until fully combined. Pour the batter into the prepared pan and bake until light golden brown and a knife inserted into the center comes out clean, 18 to 24 minutes. Let cool to room temperature, then gently invert the pan to remove the cake.

Place an 8-inch round of cardboard in the bottom of an 8 by 3-inch metal cake ring. Trim the top of the cake so that the cake is 1 inch thick and press it into the bottom of the cake ring. Top with heaping spoonfuls of the ice cream to make a 1-inch-thick layer and spread smooth with an offset spatula to remove any air pockets. Transfer the cake to the freezer for 30 minutes to set. Remove from the freezer and top with heaping spoonfuls of the sherbet to fill the cake ring and spread smooth with an offset spatula. Cover the top of the cake with plastic wrap and freeze for at least 4 hours to firmly set.

Remove the cake from the freezer and, with plastic wrap intact, invert onto a flat surface. Remove the cardboard base, invert the cake right side up onto a serving dish, and discard the plastic wrap. Use a kitchen torch to lightly warm the sides of the cake ring, or let the cake stand at room temperature until the ice cream softens slightly, and remove the cake ring. Return the cake to the freezer until ready to serve.

Just before slicing, whip the cream to soft peaks and dollop over the top of the cake. Pit and slice the remaining peach and use it to decorate the top of the cake. Serve immediately.

Sweet Corn Ice Cream

6 large egg yolks

2 ears of sweet corn, kernels cut from the cobs

1½ cups whole milk

1½ cups heavy cream

¼ teaspoon fine sea salt

½ cup plus 3 tablespoons granulated sugar, divided

PREPARE A LARGE bowl of ice water and set aside.

Put the egg yolks in a large bowl; cover with plastic wrap and set aside. In a medium saucepan, bring the corn kernels, milk, cream, salt, and ¼ cup of the sugar to a full boil. Remove from the heat and let steep for 10 minutes. Return the mixture to a full boil.

Whisk the remaining ¼ cup plus 3 tablespoons sugar into the bowl with the yolks until smooth. Gently temper the yolks by slowly adding the hot cream mixture, whisking constantly. When completely combined, strain the mixture through a fine-mesh sieve into a large metal bowl. Place the bowl of ice-cream base in the bowl of ice water and stir until cool.

Freeze the mixture in an ice-cream machine according to the manufacturer's directions until the ice cream has a smooth, soft-serve-like texture. Store in the freezer for 4 hours before serving.

Peach-Buttermilk Sherbet

3 large, ripe peaches

1⅔ cups buttermilk

3 tablespoons light corn syrup

1 cup granulated sugar

¼ teaspoon fine sea salt

PIT AND ROUGHLY chop the peaches, keeping the skin on the fruit. Puree the peaches, buttermilk, corn syrup, sugar, and salt in a blender until completely liquefied. Strain the mixture through a fine-mesh sieve into a bowl.

Freeze the mixture in an ice-cream machine according to the manufacturer's directions until the sherbet has a smooth, creamy texture. Store in the freezer for 4 hours before serving.

PLUOT PRESERVES

I have a particular fondness for pluots, a hybrid fruit that is a cross between plums and apricots. Each summer, I treat myself to a small flat by mail order from Frog Hollow Farm, my favorite northern California grower. I use its prized fruit to make jars of preserves, which I slowly ration until the following harvest. MAKES 1½ CUPS

18 small, ripe pluots

2¼ teaspoons powdered pectin

1 cup granulated sugar, divided

¼ teaspoon fine sea salt

Seeds from ½ vanilla bean

PIT AND ROUGHLY chop the pluots into large chunks. In a small bowl, combine the pectin and ¼ cup of the sugar and set aside.

In a large saucepan, combine the pluots, the remaining ¾ cup sugar, the salt, and vanilla and bring to a boil. Reduce the heat to a simmer, slowly add the pectin mixture, and stir until fully dissolved. Return the mixture to a boil and cook until the preserves just begin to thicken, about 5 minutes. Remove from the heat, transfer to a shallow heatproof dish, and let cool to room temperature. Cover and refrigerate overnight before using.

NOTE: Jam can be stored in the refrigerator for up to 3 weeks.

Plumcots, pluots, and apriums are hybrids of plums and apricots. Plumcots have been grown for hundreds of years in regions that produce both plums and apricots from seed. During the late twentieth century, California farmers, wanting to create a unique fruit, began crossbreeding the two fruits by hand-pollinating their blossoms. Plumcots, a 50/50 percent blend; pluots, a 60/40 percent blend of plum and apricot; and apriums, a 75/25 percent blend of apricot and plum, are the most common varieties available today.

PLUM-ALMOND TORTE

When plum season is at its peak, I find it difficult to choose from the many tempting varieties. Each is distinct—from sour to cloyingly sweet, in colors that range from lime green to aubergine, and in sizes as small as a grape to as large as an apple. This rustic torte is the ideal recipe for such a dilemma because it calls for several kinds of plums. Accompany the torte with my Pluot Preserves to make this dessert even more exceptional. MAKES ONE 10-INCH TORTE

Nonstick cooking spray

½ cup plus 2 tablespoons granulated sugar, plus more for the pan

¾ cup plus 1 tablespoon cake flour

¼ teaspoon fine sea salt

¼ teaspoon baking powder

¼ teaspoon baking soda

2 ounces (½ stick) unsalted butter, softened

¼ cup (2 ounces) cream cheese

½ teaspoon pure almond extract

¼ cup almond flour

3 large eggs, separated

¼ teaspoon cream of tartar

8 ripe plums, pitted and cut in half

1 tablespoon turbinado sugar

1 recipe Pluot Preserves (page 179; optional)

POSITION A RACK in the center of the oven and preheat to 350°F. Lightly coat a 10-inch fluted tart pan with nonstick cooking spray and coat lightly with sugar.

Sift the cake flour, salt, baking powder, and baking soda together into a bowl and set aside.

In the bowl of a stand mixer fitted with the paddle attachment, cream the butter, cream cheese, and granulated sugar together until smooth. Add the almond extract, almond flour, and egg yolks and mix until just combined. Scrape down the sides of the bowl, slowly add the dry ingredients, and mix until light and fluffy, 3 to 5 minutes. Transfer the batter to a large bowl.

In the clean bowl of a stand mixer fitted with the whisk attachment, beat the egg whites and cream of tartar on high speed until tripled in volume and soft but not dry peaks form. With a rubber spatula, gently fold the whipped egg whites into the batter, in two additions. Spread the batter into the prepared pan. Place plums, cut side up, on top of the batter, and sprinkle the entire surface with turbinado sugar. Bake until light golden brown and a knife inserted into the torte comes out clean, about 35 minutes.

Let the cake cool on a rack for about 20 minutes, then carefully turn the torte out of the pan onto a sheet of parchment paper, and then carefully invert right side up onto the rack to cool. Serve slices warm with a dollop of preserves (if using).

(top) Pluot Preserves, *(bottom)* Plum-Almond Torte

RICOTTA BAVARIAN WITH CANTALOUPE SOUP

Unlike many ricotta-flavored mousse recipes, the texture of this Bavarian is silky smooth. That's because the cheese is whipped in a food processor to make it incredibly soft. Served with a pool of ice-cold cantaloupe soup, a bit of fresh melon, and a few torn mint leaves, this dessert makes an elegant finale to a summer soirée. MAKES 8 SERVINGS

¼ cup plus 5 tablespoons granulated sugar, divided

3¼ teaspoons powdered gelatin

1¼ cups heavy cream, divided

2 pinches of fine sea salt, divided

1 cup (about 9 ounces) whole milk ricotta

3 large eggs, separated

1 ripe cantaloupe, peeled, seeded, and cut into small chunks, plus extra for melon balls (optional)

Juice of 1 lime

¾ cup water

Honeydew melon for melon balls (optional)

4 fresh mint sprigs, stemmed (optional)

PLACE EIGHT 4-OUNCE ramekins on a baking sheet. In a small bowl, whisk together 1 tablespoon of the sugar and the gelatin and set aside.

In the bowl of a stand mixer fitted with the whisk attachment, whip 1 cup of the cream until stiff peaks form. Transfer the cream to another bowl and refrigerate until ready to use.

Puree 2 tablespoons of the sugar, 1 pinch of salt, the ricotta, and egg yolks in a food processor until completely smooth. Meanwhile, bring the remaining ¼ cup cream to a simmer in a small saucepan. Remove from the heat, slowly add the gelatin mixture, and stir until fully dissolved. Add the gelatin mixture to the ricotta mixture in the food processor and puree until smooth, about 1 minute. Transfer the mixture to a large bowl and set aside.

In a clean bowl of a stand mixer fitted with a clean whisk attachment, beat the egg whites and 2 tablespoons of the sugar until a thick and glossy meringue forms, about 5 minutes. Add the meringue to the ricotta mixture and whisk until smooth. Gently fold in the whipped cream. Divide the mousse evenly among the ramekins, cover with plastic wrap, and freeze overnight.

To make the soup, puree the cantaloupe, lime juice, water, the remaining ¼ cup sugar, and the remaining 1 pinch of salt in a blender until liquefied. Strain the mixture through a fine-mesh sieve into a bowl and refrigerate overnight to chill. Skim away any thick puree that floats to the surface and discard. Strain the soup a second time.

When ready to serve, dip the ramekins into a bowl of hot water to loosen the mousse, run a butter knife around the edge, and invert onto serving dishes. Let stand at room temperature for a few minutes to thaw. Scoop balls from the cantaloupe and honeydew melon (if using). Serve with cantaloupe soup, and garnish with freshly torn mint leaves (if using) and a mixture of melon balls (if using).

VANILLA BEAN SEMIFREDDO WITH WARM BLACKBERRY-LIME SAUCE

Semifreddo, Italian for "semifrozen," is essentially frozen mousse. This recipe is the product of three years of tinkering. I adjusted the ratios of all the whipped ingredients until the texture and flavor became a triumph, especially when paired with the blackberry-lime sauce. MAKES 8 TO 10 SERVINGS

1¾ cups heavy cream

4 large egg yolks

¾ cup granulated sugar, divided

2 large egg whites

Seeds from 1 vanilla bean

1 recipe Warm Blackberry-Lime Sauce (recipe follows)

IN THE BOWL of a stand mixer fitted with the whisk attachment, beat the cream until stiff peaks form. Transfer the whipped cream to another bowl and refrigerate until ready to use.

In the clean bowl of the stand mixer fitted with a clean whisk attachment, beat the egg yolks and ¼ cup of the sugar on high speed until thick, glossy, and tripled in volume, about 5 minutes. Transfer the mixture to a large bowl and set aside.

In the clean bowl of the stand mixer fitted with a clean whisk attachment, beat the egg whites, the remaining ½ cup sugar, and the vanilla on high speed until thick, glossy, and tripled in volume, about 5 minutes. Gently fold the egg whites into the yolks, then gently fold in the whipped cream until evenly incorporated. Spoon the mixture into eight to ten 4-ounce ramekins or a loaf pan, cover the mousse with plastic wrap, and freeze overnight.

When ready to serve, dip the ramekins into a bowl of hot water to loosen the semifreddo, run a butter knife around the edge, and invert onto serving dishes. Garnish with a few spoonfuls of warm blackberry-lime sauce.

Warm Blackberry-Lime Sauce

1 pint blackberries

3 tablespoons granulated sugar

2 tablespoons light brown sugar

Pinch of fine sea salt

Finely grated zest of 1 lime

IN A COVERED sauté pan, bring the blackberries, granulated sugar, brown sugar, salt, and lime zest to a full boil. Remove the lid, reduce the heat to a simmer, and cook until the liquid thickens to a syrup consistency, 6 to 8 minutes.

CAVA-CHAMOMILE GELATIN
WITH FRESH RED CURRANTS

While living in Madrid, I created a fabulous brunch cocktail—a mix of iced manzanilla tea, the Spanish equivalent of chamomile, with a splash of cava, a Spanish sparkling wine. Years later I incorporated the tea and wine in this comforting dessert. The simple gelatin base lets their flavors intensify. Garnish with a few tart red currants for color.

MAKES SIX 4-OUNCE SERVINGS

½ cup superfine sugar

Pinch of fine sea salt

2 tablespoons powdered gelatin

One 750-ml bottle of cava

5 bags chamomile tea, tags removed

Juice from ½ lemon

1 pint red currants, snipped into small sprigs of berries

PLACE 6 GELATIN molds on a baking sheet or flat tray. Prepare a large bowl of ice water and set aside.

Combine the superfine sugar, salt, and gelatin in a small bowl and set aside.

In a large saucepan, bring the cava and tea bags to a boil. Turn off the heat and let the tea steep for 10 minutes. Return to a simmer and cook for 3 minutes. Remove from the heat, and discard the tea bags. Add the gelatin mixture and the lemon juice, and whisk until fully dissolved. Strain the mixture through a fine-mesh sieve into a large, heatproof bowl. Place the bowl over the prepared bowl of ice water and stir occasionally until cooled to room temperature.

Ladle the liquid into the molds and drop 2 or 3 small sprigs of currants into each mold. Lightly cover with plastic wrap and carefully transfer the gelatins to the refrigerator. Chill overnight to set.

To unmold the gelatins, dip the molds in hot water to loosen, run a knife along the edge, and invert directly onto individual serving dishes. If you have difficulty unmolding the gelatins, hide any imperfections with a few extra currants or a dollop of whipped cream.

ESPRESSO GRANITA WITH COCOA CREAM

My easy granita recipe requires occasional stirring over a few hours, even while it is setting in the freezer. This extra attention helps the granita to form large ice crystals that shave nicely. Make this dessert on a Saturday morning, with leftover coffee. Freeze overnight; it will be ready in time for Sunday brunch. MAKES 8 SERVINGS

3 cups freshly brewed coffee

2 shots freshly brewed espresso, or 2 teaspoons instant espresso powder

⅓ cup superfine sugar

Pinch of fine sea salt

¾ cup heavy cream

2 tablespoons confectioners' sugar

3 tablespoons cocoa powder

Cocoa powder or chocolate shavings (optional)

COMBINE THE COFFEE, espresso, superfine sugar, and salt in a large mixing bowl and whisk until the sugar is dissolved. Pour the mixture into a shallow dish and freeze overnight, stirring every hour for the first 3 hours of freezing to help ice crystals form.

Just before serving, place serving glasses in the freezer for a few minutes to chill. Meanwhile, for cocoa whipped cream, beat the cream, confectioners' sugar, and cocoa until soft peaks have formed; set aside.

Scrape the granita with a fork, breaking up any large pieces that may remain in the bottom of the dish. Gently spoon the granita into the glasses and top with a dollop of cocoa whipped cream. Garnish with a pinch of cocoa powder or chocolate shavings (if using).

CHOCOLATE–PEANUT BUTTER S'MORES

My sophisticated take on this popular summertime dessert won me a mention in Sam Sifton's *New York Times* three-star review of Craft, Tom Colicchio's beloved farm-to-table restaurant in Manhattan. The smoked salt gives these made-at-home s'mores a toasty, campfire flavor. MAKES 8 SERVINGS

For the chocolate-peanut butter mousse:

1½ cups heavy cream

½ cup plus 2 tablespoons confectioners' sugar

1 cup (about 6 ounces) semisweet chocolate chips

½ cup creamy peanut butter

¼ cup plus 2 tablespoons (3 ounces) cream cheese

For the marshmallow meringue:

3 large egg whites

Seeds from ½ vanilla bean

1 tablespoon plus 1 cup granulated sugar, divided

½ cup water

1 tablespoon light corn syrup

Pinch of fine sea salt

To assemble:

16 Homemade Graham Crackers (page 226)

½ to 1 teaspoon smoked sea salt

MAKE THE CHOCOLATE–PEANUT butter mousse: Line an 8-inch square pan with parchment paper.

In the bowl of a stand mixer fitted with the whisk attachment, beat the cream and confectioners' sugar until medium peaks form. Transfer the whipped cream to a small bowl and refrigerate until ready to use.

Using a double boiler, melt the chocolate chips over a very low heat. Remove from the heat and let stand until ready to use.

Using the same bowl of a stand mixer fitted with the paddle attachment, cream the peanut butter and cream cheese until just combined. Slowly add the melted chocolate and mix until smooth, scraping down the sides of the bowl as needed. Switch back to the whisk attachment, add the whipped cream, and beat the entire mixture on high speed until completely smooth, about 1 minute, to create a mousse.

Spread the mousse into the prepared pan, cover the surface directly with a sheet of plastic wrap, and refrigerate until very firm, about 2 hours. Once completely chilled, cut the mousse into 2½-inch squares using a sharp knife dipped in hot water.

Make the marshmallow meringue: In the bowl of a stand mixer fitted with the whisk attachment, beat the egg whites, vanilla, and 1 tablespoon of the sugar on low speed. Meanwhile, combine the remaining 1 cup sugar, the water, corn syrup, and salt in a small saucepan and cook over medium heat until the mixture reaches 238°F on a candy thermometer. Remove from the heat, increase the speed of the mixer to medium-high, and very slowly pour the hot sugar mixture over the egg whites, taking care not to pour the mixture onto the moving whisk. Increase the speed of the mixer to high and whip until tripled in volume, thick, glossy, and cooled to room temperature. Refrigerate until ready to use.

To assemble, place a graham cracker on a serving dish. Top with a square of mousse, spoon a large dollop of meringue over the mousse, and brown using a hand-held kitchen torch until deep golden brown. Sprinkle with a pinch of smoked salt and top with another graham cracker. Repeat the steps with the remaining components to make 7 more s'mores and serve immediately.

NOTE: This recipe has several components. To make the prep go smoothly, first prepare the dough for the graham crackers. While it is chilling, make the chocolate–peanut butter mousse. Once the dough has been rolled, cut into squares, and is baking in the oven, turn your attention to the marshmallow meringue. Assemble the s'mores just before serving.

NUTELLA-RASPBERRY CRÊPES

Any excuse to eat Nutella is a good one for me. When lightened with mascarpone, it makes a satisfying crêpe filling. Perfect for a weekend brunch, these crêpes can be prepared a couple of hours in advance. Decorate with fresh raspberries and chopped hazelnuts just before serving. MAKES 8 SERVINGS

¾ cup (about 3¾ ounces) hazelnuts, coarsely chopped

1 cup (8 ounces) mascarpone

2 cups (16 ounces) Nutella

1 recipe Cocoa Crêpes (page 227)

1½ pints raspberries

POSITION A RACK in the center of the oven and preheat to 350°F.

Spread the hazelnuts on a baking sheet and bake until golden and fragrant, about 8 minutes. Let cool to room temperature.

In a large bowl, fold the mascarpone and Nutella together until smooth.

To serve, dollop 2 or 3 tablespoons of the filling onto the center of each crêpe, top with 5 or 6 raspberries, then sprinkle with 1½ teaspoons of the hazelnuts and gently fold the crêpe in half twice. Arrange the crêpes on a serving dish and garnish with the remaining raspberries and hazelnuts.

BLACKBERRY BLINTZES

My mother introduced me to her favorite Polish dish, twice-cooked pancakes called *nalesniki*. When I was little, she would sometimes let me skip pierogis and kielbasa for dinner and as a treat have these fruit-and-cheese-filled pancakes instead. Now that I live in New York, I call my recipe by the more common name blintz. These blintzes make a light warm-weather dessert, especially when paired with fresh blackberries.

MAKES 8 SERVINGS

¾ cup (about 7 ounces) whole milk ricotta

¼ cup (2 ounces) cream cheese, softened

3 tablespoons confectioners' sugar

Seeds from ½ vanilla bean

Juice of ½ lemon

2 pinches of fine sea salt, divided

1½ pints whole blackberries, plus 24 more blackberries, cut in half, divided

3 tablespoons granulated sugar

Finely grated zest of ¼ lemon

¼ cup water

1 recipe Vanilla Bean Crêpes (page 227)

Nonstick cooking spray

IN THE BOWL of a stand mixer fitted with the paddle attachment, cream the ricotta, cream cheese, confectioners' sugar, vanilla, lemon juice, and 1 pinch of salt until evenly combined. Set aside until ready to use.

For the blackberry sauce, in a small saucepan, combine the whole blackberries, granulated sugar, lemon zest, water, and the remaining pinch of salt and simmer over medium heat until the liquid is reduced by half, about 8 minutes. Remove from the heat and let stand until ready to use.

On a large clean surface, lay each crêpe flat, lighter side facing up, and place about 1 tablespoon of the ricotta filling and 3 blackberry halves in the center. Fold each crêpe in thirds (like a business letter) to cover the filling, then fold each side inward to seal and create a small square-shaped blintz.

Lightly coat a large nonstick sauté pan with nonstick cooking spray and warm over medium heat. Place 4 blintzes in the pan and cook until light golden brown, about 2 minutes on each side. Serve warm, garnished with a few spoonfuls of the warm blackberry sauce. Repeat with the remaining blintzes.

FUNNEL CAKES

A funnel cake's freshly deep-fried batter, doused in confectioners' sugar, is over the top. So why wait for the state fair or a carnival to come to town to enjoy one? My recipe is quick to make at home. MAKES 30 FUNNEL CAKES

2 ⅔ cups unbleached all-purpose flour

2 teaspoons baking powder

½ teaspoon fine sea salt

2 large eggs

⅓ cup granulated sugar

⅓ cup packed light brown sugar

1 ⅓ cups whole milk

¾ teaspoon pure vanilla extract

Canola oil for frying

Confectioners' sugar for dusting

LINE A LARGE platter with paper towels. Fit a pastry bag with a ¼-inch round pastry tip.

Sift the flour, baking powder, and salt into a large bowl. Add the eggs, granulated sugar, brown sugar, milk, and vanilla and whisk until completely smooth. Transfer the batter to the prepared pastry bag, being sure to fold the tip of the bag closed to prevent the batter from leaking, and set aside to rest for 15 minutes.

Over medium-high heat, bring a large skillet filled with 2 to 2½ inches of oil to 375°F on a deep-frying thermometer.

Carefully pipe the batter into 6 to 8 rosettes or spirals, about 3 inches in diameter, over the surface of the oil. Fry the funnel cakes until deep golden brown, about 2 minutes on each side. Using a slotted spoon or skimmer, remove the cakes from the oil and place them on the prepared platter to drain. Repeat with the remaining batter, increasing or lowering the heat to keep the temperature of the oil at 375°F. Dust with confectioners' sugar just before serving.

(left) Funnel Cakes, *(right)* Warm Peach Hand Pies

WARM PEACH HAND PIES

Stories about the merits of the state of Alabama's peaches abound—locals claim they are even better than the Georgia variety. In fact, each McCoy summer family reunion ends with a visit to Demetri's in Homewood for handmade, fried-to-order peach hand pies, washed down with a glass of sweet tea. My version of these wonderful hand pies brings forth the peachiness of this juicy summer fruit. MAKES 14 TO 16 PIES

4 ripe peaches, pitted and cut into ½-inch cubes

¼ teaspoon fine sea salt

¾ cup granulated sugar

Unbleached all-purpose flour for rolling

1 recipe Perfect Pie Dough (page 225)

1 large egg, lightly beaten

Canola oil for frying

2 cups White Icing (page 231)

IN A MEDIUM saucepan, bring the peaches, salt, and sugar to a boil over high heat, stirring frequently. Reduce the heat to medium-low and simmer until the fruit softens and the liquid thickens, 15 to 20 minutes. Return to a full boil for 3 to 5 minutes to thicken the liquid further. Transfer the mixture to a shallow heatproof dish and refrigerate until cool.

Line two baking sheets with parchment paper. Have 2 extra sheets of parchment paper cut and set aside.

On a lightly floured surface, roll one disk of dough into a large rectangle by starting at the center of the disk and rolling away from you. Use additional flour and give the dough a quarter turn between each roll to prevent it from sticking to the table. Continue rolling until the dough is an even ⅛ inch thick. Repeat with the remaining disk of dough, refrigerating the first sheet of dough as you roll the second. Place the second sheet of dough in the refrigerator.

Cut 4-inch circles from both sheets of the pie dough, arrange the circles on one prepared baking sheet, layering the remaining sheets of parchment paper between the circles. Refrigerate the dough until firm, about 20 minutes.

Remove the circles of dough from the refrigerator, 2 at a time, and place on a lightly floured surface. Place 1 tablespoon of the peach filling onto the center of each circle. Lightly brush the edges of the circles with beaten egg and carefully fold in half. Using your fingertips dipped in flour, firmly pinch the edges of the dough together to seal closed (*figs. 1 and 2*). Then, using the tines of a fork, firmly press into the sealed edges of the hand pies to decorate. Transfer the assembled pies to the second prepared baking sheet and refrigerate immediately. Continue with the remaining hand pies until all of them are filled. Transfer the pies to the freezer until the dough is firm, about 20 minutes.

Over medium-high heat, bring a large skillet filled with 2 to 2½ inches of oil to 375°F on a deep-frying thermometer. Line a large platter with paper towels.

Carefully place about 6 pies into the oil. Fry until deep golden brown, turning in the oil as needed, 7 to 8 minutes. Using a slotted spoon or skimmer, remove the pies from the oil and let them drain on the prepared platter until just warm or room temperature.

Using a teaspoon, drizzle the pies decoratively with icing, or gently brush the icing over the entire surface of the pies with a pastry brush. Let the icing set for 5 to 10 minutes before serving.

NOTE: Unbaked pies can be frozen for a later day. If wrapped tightly in a freezer bag and aluminum foil, they will last 2 to 3 months. When ready to serve, drop them frozen solid into hot frying oil, giving them a few extra minutes to warm all the way through.

Halfway between Birmingham and Montgomery, in the small town of Clanton, stands a giant water tower whose round reservoir is painted as a giant peach, complete with a stem and leaf. This is a fun roadside attraction and a reminder to brake at the next farmers' stand just off I-65 before heading farther south.

1   2

PROSECCO SABAYON AND FRESH STONE FRUIT

Sabayon is a cross between a mousse and custardy sauce, an elegant accompaniment to fresh or roasted fruit. My sabayon recipe is quick to make. The prosecco can be replaced with other varieties of wine or liquor—rum in autumn or winter is a personal favorite.

MAKES 8 TO 10 SERVINGS

5 large egg yolks

½ cup prosecco

½ cup wildflower honey, divided

Pinch of fine sea salt, plus more for garnishing

½ cup heavy cream

3 ripe peaches

3 ripe nectarines

6 ripe apricots

3 ripe yellow plums

3 ripe red plums

IN A MEDIUM saucepan, bring about 2 inches of water to a simmer. Prepare a large bowl of ice water and set aside.

Whisk the egg yolks, prosecco, ¼ cup of the honey, and the salt together in a large heatproof bowl that is a few inches wider than the saucepan. Place the bowl over the simmering water and cook, whisking constantly, until thickened, light in color, and a thermometer reads 165°F, 8 to 10 minutes. Place the bowl of sabayon over the bowl of ice water and stir occasionally until cooled to room temperature.

In the bowl of a stand mixer fitted with the whisk attachment, beat the cream until stiff peaks form. Gently fold the whipped cream into the sabayon, cover the bowl with plastic wrap, and refrigerate until cool.

When ready to serve, cut the peaches, nectarines, apricots, yellow plums, and red plums in half, remove the pits, and slice into a variety of thicknesses. Divide the sabayon evenly among serving dishes, arrange a mixture of fruit slices on each plate, drizzle with the remaining ¼ cup honey, and garnish with a pinch of salt.

NOTE: Another option is grilling the stone fruit. Toss the sliced fruit in a few tablespoons of extra-virgin olive oil and grill over high heat until just tender and nicely marked, a few minutes on each side. Serve the grilled fruit warm or at room temperature alongside the sabayon.

RASPBERRY-CHOCOLATE CHIP BUNDT CAKE

Bundt cake, derived from the German ring-shaped teatime cake called *Bundkuchen*, is relatively easy to make. My batter, dotted with fresh raspberries and chocolate chips, is whipped up in one bowl; the decorative pan and simple glaze of chocolate ganache do all the work to give it a festive appearance. MAKES ONE 9½-INCH CAKE

Nonstick cooking spray

2½ cups unbleached all-purpose flour

2 teaspoons baking powder

8 ounces (2 sticks) unsalted butter, softened

1 cup packed light brown sugar

¾ cup granulated sugar

½ teaspoon fine sea salt

1 teaspoon pure vanilla extract

4 large eggs

1 cup sour cream

2 tablespoons heavy cream

1½ cups (about 9 ounces) semisweet chocolate chips

1½ pints raspberries

1 recipe Semisweet Chocolate Ganache (page 229)

POSITION A RACK in the bottom of the oven and preheat to 325°F. Place a cooling rack over a parchment-lined baking sheet. Lightly coat a 9½-inch Bundt pan with nonstick cooking spray.

Sift the flour and baking powder together into a bowl and set aside.

In the bowl of a stand mixer fitted with the paddle attachment, cream the butter, brown sugar, granulated sugar, and salt until light and fluffy, about 5 minutes. Add the vanilla and eggs, one at a time, and mix until just incorporated. Scrape down the sides of the bowl, add the dry ingredients, and mix until smooth. Add the sour cream and heavy cream and mix until perfectly smooth. Remove the bowl from the mixer and gently fold in the chocolate chips and raspberries until evenly dispersed.

Spoon the batter evenly into the prepared pan. Bake until deep golden brown and a knife inserted into the center of the cake comes out clean, about 1 hour. Let the cake cool in the pan for 20 minutes, then carefully invert onto the prepared cooling rack.

Slowly pour the warm ganache evenly over the top of the cake, allowing the excess to drip down the sides. Let the ganache set for 15 to 20 minutes before transferring the cake to a serving plate and slicing.

NOTES: The key to making this cake a success is to use a heavy-duty aluminum Bundt cake pan, preferably with a nonstick coating. Much like a pound cake, a Bundt cake batter is dense and takes a while to bake. Do not use a lightweight pan because the heat from the oven will transfer too easily through its thin sides and produce a cake that is baked in the center but burned to a crisp on the edges. For best results, I recommend a Bundt pan made by Nordic Ware (see Resource Guide, page 234).

Begin making the semisweet chocolate ganache after the cake has cooled so you can pour the ganache over the cooled cake while it is still warm and liquid.

RASPBERRY–CRÈME FRAÎCHE TARTS

Dainty berry tartlets served with a tall glass of sun tea are a lovely treat on a warm summer afternoon. Make the effort to visit your farmers' market to hand-select the finest raspberries available, and be sure to use local cream for the Homemade Crème Fraîche.

MAKES TEN TO TWELVE 4-INCH TARTLETS

Nonstick cooking spray

Unbleached all-purpose flour for rolling

1 recipe Blonde Sablé Dough (page 224)

1 cup Homemade Crème Fraîche (page 230)

¼ cup heavy cream

3 tablespoons granulated sugar

Pinch of fine sea salt

1½ pints raspberries

¼ cup (about 1 ounce) pistachios, roughly chopped

POSITION A RACK in the center of the oven and preheat to 350°F. Lightly coat 10 to 12 tartlet pans with nonstick cooking spray and place on a baking sheet.

On a lightly floured surface, roll one disk of the dough into a large rectangle by starting at the center of the disk and rolling away from you. Use additional flour and give the dough a quarter turn between each roll to prevent it from sticking to the table. Continue rolling until the dough is an even ⅛ inch thick. Repeat with the remaining disk of dough, refrigerating the first sheet of dough as you roll the second. Place the second sheet of dough in the refrigerator.

Cut 5-inch circles from the first sheet of dough and carefully line the tartlet pans, pressing the dough evenly into the interior corners of each pan. Trim away the excess dough from the edge of each shell with the back of a knife. Repeat with the second sheet of dough. Freeze the shells until fully hardened, about 15 minutes.

Bake the shells until light golden brown, 16 to 18 minutes. Rotate the baking sheet midway through the baking time, and pierce gently with the tines of a fork if the centers of the shells puff. Let cool to room temperature.

Just before serving, whip the crème fraîche, cream, sugar, and salt together in a large bowl until thickened. Fill each tartlet shell full with the whipped crème fraîche and top with the raspberries and chopped pistachios.

RASPBERRY-LAVENDER FLOATS

After purchasing a flat of the season's sweetest raspberries from the farmers' market, I decided to experiment by tasting a fresh raspberry with a leaf of every variety of herb in my garden—basil, thyme, cilantro, rosemary, and lavender—to come up with a new flavor combination. The lavender pairing was the best, so I topped my Lavender Ice Cream with homemade raspberry soda to make this refreshing float. MAKES 8 TO 10 SERVINGS

2 pints raspberries

1¼ cups superfine sugar

1¼ cups cold water

Pinch of fine sea salt

3 cups soda water

1 recipe Lavender Ice Cream (page 232)

PUREE THE RASPBERRIES, superfine sugar, water, and salt in a blender until completely liquefied. Strain the mixture through a fine-mesh sieve into a bowl, using a spoon to push all the liquid through, and discard the seeds and pulp in the sieve.

Just before serving, slowly add the soda water to the bowl of raspberry puree and gently stir to combine. Take care not to overmix, or the soda will go flat. Fill each glass with 2 or 3 scoops of ice cream, top with the raspberry soda, and serve immediately.

NOTE: When raspberries are at the peak of their season, remember to throw a few pints into freezer bags and store them for the winter. There is nothing more exciting than uncovering a bit of summer on a dreary winter day.

RED CURRANT CLAFOUTIS

Whenever I am asked, "What is your favorite dessert to bake?," my answer is always clafoutis. It is a classic French dessert that is deceptively easy to prepare. Just like a soufflé, clafoutis rises to an impressive height and must be served directly from the oven. Sour cherries are the traditional choice during the warmer months, but for my summer clafoutis, I prefer tart red currants. MAKES 8 SERVINGS

2 tablespoons unsalted butter, melted, plus more for the pan

1/4 cup granulated sugar, plus more for the pan

1/2 cup unbleached all-purpose flour

Pinch of fine sea salt

3 large eggs

2 large egg yolks

3/4 cup plus 1 tablespoon heavy cream

Seeds from 1 vanilla bean

Finely grated zest of 1 lemon

1 1/2 cups red currants, stems removed

1/3 cup (about 1 1/2 ounces) pistachios, roughly chopped

1 tablespoon turbinado sugar

POSITION A RACK in the center of the oven and preheat to 350°F. Lightly butter and sugar a 9-inch glass, ceramic, or cast-iron pie plate.

In a large bowl, combine the flour, granulated sugar, and salt. Add the whole eggs, egg yolks, cream, vanilla, and lemon zest and whisk until perfectly smooth. Slowly whisk in the melted butter. Pour the batter into the prepared pie plate, scatter the currants over the top, and sprinkle with the pistachios and turbinado sugar.

Place the pie plate on a baking sheet and bake for 15 minutes. Increase the oven temperature to 375°F and continue to bake until puffed, set in the center, and light golden brown, another 25 to 30 minutes. Serve immediately from the oven.

NOTE: The batter can be made and refrigerated in advance of baking for up to 3 days.

NUTTY MERINGUES

While most would advise making meringue in the winter months because summer's humidity can prevent these cookies from staying crisp, I can't help but break the rule. This confection's light and airy texture, intensely packed with nuts, is perfect during summer if you desire a sweet treat that won't weigh you down. As soon as they are at room temperature, pop them into an airtight container and store them in a cool, dry place in your kitchen. MAKES ABOUT 30 COOKIES

¾ cup unsweetened shredded coconut

¼ cup (about 1¼ ounces) whole hazelnuts

¼ cup (about 1 ounce) sliced almonds

2 large egg whites

1 cup plus 2 tablespoons confectioners' sugar

Pinch of fine sea salt

¼ teaspoon pure almond extract

½ teaspoon pure vanilla extract

POSITION TWO RACKS in the center of the oven and preheat to 350°F. Line two baking sheets with silicone baking mats.

Spread the coconut, hazelnuts, and almonds on a prepared baking sheet and toast until light golden brown, 6 to 8 minutes. Let cool completely to room temperature. Transfer the coconut-nut mixture to a large cutting board and roughly chop the nuts into smaller pieces; set aside. Reserve the baking sheets and silicone mats for later use.

In the bowl of a stand mixer fitted with the whisk attachment, beat the egg whites, confectioners' sugar, salt, almond extract, and vanilla on high speed until thick, glossy, stiff peaks form, about 8 minutes. Gently fold the coconut-nut mixture into the meringue in two additions. Spoon heaping teaspoons of the batter onto the prepared baking sheets, about 1 inch in diameter and about 1 inch apart. Bake until light golden brown and the surfaces crack, about 10 minutes. Let cool to room temperature.

NOTES: The best way to neatly shape cookies from this sticky batter is to use two teaspoons: one spoon for scooping the batter and a second for pushing the batter onto the baking sheet.

Meringues can be stored in an airtight container for up to 3 days.

(left and right) Plum–Poppy Seed *Kolache*, Nutty Meringues

PLUM–POPPY SEED *KOLACHE*

My grandmother Charlotte's favorite pastime was spending dough at Las Vegas's blackjack tables. But every Christmas, she'd don an apron and roll out dough of a different kind. Her baking was an entertaining spectacle—coming from the kitchen we would hear cries of profanity, the lighting of cigarettes, and the tinkling of ice cubes in her cocktail glass. Muffling our laughter, we did not dare interfere. Those cookie recipes, on notecards originally written in Bohemian, were passed down from generation to generation. This variation of Plum–Poppy Seed *Kolache* is my way of remembering that she wasn't always one tough cookie. MAKES ABOUT 36 COOKIES

8 ounces (2 sticks) unsalted butter, softened

1 cup (8 ounces) cream cheese, softened

3 tablespoons confectioners' sugar

2 cups unbleached all-purpose flour, plus more for rolling

½ teaspoon fine sea salt

¼ cup poppy seeds

1 large egg, lightly beaten

1 recipe Plum-Cardamom Jam (recipe follows)

IN THE BOWL of a stand mixer fitted with the paddle attachment, cream the butter, cream cheese, and confectioners' sugar until combined. Add the flour, salt, and poppy seeds and continue to mix until the dough just comes together. Remove the dough from the mixer, divide it in half, and flatten each piece into a 1-inch-thick disk. Wrap them tightly in plastic wrap. Refrigerate until firm, about 2 hours.

Position a rack in the center of the oven and preheat to 375°F. Line two baking sheets with parchment paper.

On a lightly floured surface, roll one disk of the dough into a large rectangle by starting at the center of the disk and rolling away from you. Use additional flour and give the dough a quarter turn between each roll to prevent it from sticking to the table. Continue rolling until the dough is an even ⅛ inch thick. Repeat with the remaining disk of dough, refrigerating the first sheet of dough as you roll the second. Place the second sheet of dough in the refrigerator.

Cut 2½-inch squares from the first sheet of dough and set them on the prepared baking sheets. Lightly brush the dough squares with beaten egg and place about 1½ teaspoons of jam on the center of each square.

To shape the cookies, bring 2 opposite corners of the dough together and firmly pinch to seal just at the tips of each corner. Repeat with the remaining 2 corners, pinching firmly to seal all 4 tips together, to create a small pyramid-shaped pouch. Freeze the cookies for about 15 minutes to harden them before baking.

Bake the cookies until light golden brown, about 20 minutes. Let cool on the baking sheets to room temperature.

NOTE: *Kolache* can be stored in an airtight container for up to 3 days.

Plum-Cardamom Jam

2 tablespoons plus ¼ cup
granulated sugar, divided

2 teaspoons powdered pectin

12 ripe Italian plums

¼ teaspoon fine sea salt

Generous pinch of ground
cardamom

Juice of ½ lemon

COMBINE 2 TABLESPOONS of the sugar and the pectin in a small bowl and set aside. Pit and roughly chop the plums, keeping the skin on the fruit. Puree the plums in a blender until smooth.

Transfer the plum puree to a small saucepan. Add the remaining ¼ cup sugar, the salt, and cardamom and bring to a boil for 1 minute. Slowly add the pectin mixture, stir until fully dissolved, and continue to boil until just thickened, about 8 minutes. Remove from the heat, stir in the lemon juice, transfer the jam to a shallow heatproof dish, and let cool to room temperature. Cover and refrigerate until cold before using, about 4 hours.

NOTE: Jam can be stored in the refrigerator for up to 3 weeks.

SICILIAN SPUMONI SANDWICHES

I like spumoni, an Italian frozen dessert layered with chocolate, pistachio, and cherry ice creams, best prepared Sicilian style—sandwiched in the center of a sweet brioche bun. The buns are perfect for catching drips on a hot summer day. Here is my recipe for a novel spin on America's ice-cream sandwich. MAKES ABOUT 16 SERVINGS

1 recipe Honey Brioche Dough (page 223)

Unbleached all-purpose flour for rolling

Nonstick cooking spray

1½ quarts Sweet Cream Ice Cream, softened (page 232)

¾ cup (about 5 ounces) bittersweet chocolate, roughly chopped into chunks

¾ cup (about 3 ounces) shelled pistachios, roughly chopped

¾ cup brandied cherries, roughly chopped

1 large egg, lightly beaten

2 to 3 tablespoons pearl sugar

LINE TWO BAKING sheets with parchment paper. Place three medium bowls in the freezer.

Turn the dough out onto a lightly floured surface and press into a flat disk. Cut the dough in half, and then cut each half into 8 small pieces. Gently roll each piece of dough into a small ball. Arrange the balls of dough on the prepared baking sheets, with the smoothest side facing up. Lightly coat the dough with nonstick cooking spray, cover loosely with plastic wrap, and let rise until nearly doubled in size, about 1 hour.

Divide the ice cream among the three chilled bowls. Add the chocolate chunks to one bowl, the pistachios to the second, and the cherries to the third, and stir each very quickly to combine the flavorings into the ice cream. Return the bowls of ice cream to the freezer to harden.

Position a rack in the center of the oven and preheat to 450°F.

Remove the plastic wrap from the baking sheets, gently brush the tops and sides of the rolls with the beaten egg, and generously sprinkle them with pearl sugar. Reduce the oven temperature to 375°F and bake until deep golden brown, 16 to 18 minutes. Let cool on wire racks to room temperature.

To assemble the ice-cream sandwiches, split each brioche roll in half and fill each roll with 1 large scoop of chocolate chunk, pistachio, or cherry ice cream. Eat immediately, or freeze for up to 30 minutes before serving.

Bronte, Sicily—Italy's "Capital of Pistachios"—is known for a variety of pistachios that cannot be cultivated elsewhere. This town produces merely 1 percent of the world's pistachio crop, but it is highly prized over the rest. Bronte pistachios have an exquisite flavor and are a gorgeous bright green and gold. If you want to splurge, I suggest you try them in this recipe—they will make quite a difference (see Resource Guide, page 234).

MARKET BERRY SUMMER PUDDING

I discovered summer pudding in Pastry Chef David Lebovitz's first cookbook, *Room for Dessert*. Its gorgeous color and perfectly arranged layers of bread and berries captivated me. David, formerly of Chez Panisse, is a master at making desserts from the market's bounty. My recipe is loosely based on his creation, and includes lemon verbena to give it an unusual twist. MAKES 8 SERVINGS

16 slices firm white sandwich bread

1 tablespoon plus 1 cup granulated sugar, divided

½ teaspoon powdered pectin

1 pint raspberries

1 pint blackberries

1 pint blueberries

4 sprigs fresh lemon verbena

¼ teaspoon fine sea salt

Seeds from ½ vanilla bean

Juice of 1 lemon

1 cup Whipped Mascarpone (page 230; optional)

LINE 8 RAMEKINS with plastic wrap, allowing the edges of the plastic wrap to hang over the edge of each dish. Using a round cookie cutter, cut a disk of bread from each slice to fit the interior diameter of the ramekins. Set the disks of bread aside. Combine 1 tablespoon of the sugar and the pectin in a small bowl and set aside.

In a large saucepan, combine the raspberries, blackberries, blueberries, lemon verbena, the remaining 1 cup sugar, the salt, and vanilla and cook over high heat until the berries just begin to break down. Slowly add the pectin mixture and stir until fully dissolved. Pour the berry mixture into a heatproof bowl and stir in the lemon juice. Remove the lemon verbena sprigs and discard.

Spoon 2 tablespoons of the warm berries into each ramekin *(fig.1)* and place a disk of bread on top. Spoon 2 more tablespoons of berries over the bread in each ramekin and cover with another disk of bread. Divide the remaining berries among the ramekins. Fold the overhang of plastic wrap on top of each ramekin to cover, gently pressing the puddings down to release any air bubbles. Refrigerate the puddings overnight to set.

To serve, peel away the plastic wrap from the tops of the puddings and invert the puddings directly onto serving dishes. Remove the ramekins and discard the plastic wrap. Serve the puddings with a dollop of whipped mascarpone (if using).

1

WATERMELON ICE WITH LIME CREAM

During late summer and into early fall, watermelon is at its prime. This cold and refreshing shaved ice is made with fresh fruit puree and topped with a dollop of lime whipped cream. It is my grown-up version of a snow cone. MAKES 8 TO 10 SERVINGS

One 4- to 5-pound seedless baby watermelon

½ cup superfine sugar

¼ teaspoon fine sea salt

1 cup heavy cream

1 tablespoon confectioners' sugar

Finely grated zest of 1 lime

Granulated sugar (optional)

CHOP THE WATERMELON into small chunks and discard the rinds. Puree the watermelon, superfine sugar, and salt in a blender until completely liquefied, dividing the ingredients into two batches if necessary. Strain the mixture through a fine-mesh sieve into a shallow dish, and freeze overnight, stirring every hour for the first 3 hours to help ice crystals form.

Just before serving, place 8 to 10 glasses in the freezer for a few minutes to chill. Meanwhile, for the lime whipped cream, beat the cream, confectioners' sugar, and lime zest until soft peaks have formed and set aside.

Scrape the watermelon ice with a fork, breaking up any large pieces that may remain in the bottom of the dish. Rim the glasses with granulated sugar (if using). Gently spoon the fruit ice into the glasses and garnish each with a dollop of lime whipped cream.

WHITE PEACH AND HUCKLEBERRY CRISP

Crisps are crowd-pleasers. In the height of summer, when stone fruit is at its peak, I make mine with white peaches and huckleberries for barbecues and picnics. You can serve crisps many ways—straight from the oven, at room temperature, with a scoop of ice cream, or a dollop of whipped cream. MAKES 14 SERVINGS

16 large, ripe white peaches

1 pint fresh or frozen huckleberries, stems removed

½ cup packed light brown sugar

½ cup granulated sugar

¼ cup cornstarch

¾ teaspoon fine sea salt

Seeds from 1 vanilla bean

1 recipe Oatmeal Streusel (page 228)

POSITION A RACK in the center of the oven and preheat to 325°F. Line a baking sheet with parchment paper or aluminum foil.

Pit and chop the peaches into 1-inch pieces, keeping the skin on the fruit, and place them in a large bowl. Add the huckleberries, brown sugar, granulated sugar, cornstarch, salt, and vanilla, and mix until well combined. Spread the mixture in a 9 by 13-inch baking dish and evenly top with streusel.

Place the crisp on the prepared baking sheet and bake until golden brown and the filling begins to bubble, 50 to 60 minutes. Let cool until just warm before serving.

Basics

HONEY BRIOCHE DOUGH

My brioche dough includes the addition of orange blossom water and vanilla bean. They give this rich yeasted bread an exquisite flavor. MAKES ABOUT 1½ POUNDS DOUGH

2¼ teaspoons active dry yeast

¼ cup whole milk,
warmed to about 110°F

Pinch of granulated sugar

3 large eggs

1 large egg yolk

2¼ cups plus 2 tablespoons
unbleached all-purpose flour,
divided

1½ teaspoons fine sea salt

2 tablespoons honey

1 teaspoon orange
blossom water

Seeds from ½ vanilla bean

7 ounces (1¾ sticks) cold
unsalted butter, cubed

IN THE BOWL of a stand mixer fitted with the paddle attachment, combine the yeast, milk, and sugar and let stand for about 5 minutes. Add the whole eggs, egg yolk, 2¼ cups of the flour, the salt, honey, orange blossom water, and vanilla and mix on low speed until the dough just comes together, about 1 minute. Slowly add the butter and mix until no lumps of butter remain in the dough, about 10 minutes.

Scrape down the sides of the bowl, replace the paddle with the dough hook attachment, increase the speed of the mixer to medium, and mix until the dough comes together into a smooth and shiny ball that no longer sticks to the side of the bowl, about 10 minutes. Add the remaining 2 tablespoons flour and continue to mix until well incorporated, about 2 minutes.

Turn the dough out of the bowl onto a lightly floured table and knead for about 5 minutes. Return the dough to the mixing bowl, cover with plastic wrap, and refrigerate to proof overnight.

BLONDE SABLÉ DOUGH

This sugary dough makes a lovely tart or piecrust. The dough mixes very quickly and is easy to work with; it holds its shape perfectly, even when baked without a filling; and best of all, the scraps can be rolled a second time without becoming overworked.

MAKES ENOUGH FOR TWO 9-INCH PIECRUSTS OR 12 INDIVIDUAL TARTLETS

9 ounces (2¼ sticks) unsalted butter, softened

¾ cup plus 2 tablespoons granulated sugar

2 large eggs

3¾ cups unbleached all-purpose flour

¼ teaspoon fine sea salt

IN THE BOWL of a stand mixer fitted with the paddle attachment, mix the butter and sugar on the lowest speed just until evenly combined, about 1 minute. Add the eggs and continue to mix until evenly combined, about 1 minute. Scrape down the sides of the bowl, add the flour and salt, and mix until the dough is smooth and just comes together.

Remove the dough from the mixer, divide it in half, and flatten each piece into a 1-inch thick disk. Wrap them tightly in plastic wrap, and refrigerate until firm, 1 to 2 hours.

PERFECT PIE DOUGH

The ideal method for making pie dough has been an endless conversation between my father and me. He insists that he cannot make a light and flaky crust; I believe he overthinks the process. So I created this foolproof recipe with my father in mind. This dough has a delicate consistency, but is durable enough to stand up to over mixing, rolling with too much flour, or other common mishaps. MAKES ENOUGH FOR ONE 9-INCH DOUBLE-CRUST PIE OR FOURTEEN TO SIXTEEN 4-INCH HAND PIES

3¼ cups unbleached all-purpose flour

1¼ teaspoons granulated sugar

1¼ teaspoons fine sea salt

9 ounces (2¼ sticks) cold unsalted butter, cut into ½-inch pieces

½ cup ice-cold water

1 tablespoon distilled white vinegar

IN THE BOWL of a stand mixer fitted with the paddle attachment, mix the flour, sugar, and salt on the lowest speed for a few seconds. Slowly add the butter and continue to mix until sandy and the butter is reduced to small pieces about the size of peas and marbles, about 2 minutes. Slowly add the water and vinegar and mix until the dough just comes together.

Remove the dough from the mixer, divide it in half, and flatten each piece into a 1-inch thick disk. Wrap them tightly in plastic wrap, and refrigerate until firm, 1 to 2 hours.

HOMEMADE GRAHAM CRACKERS

Homemade graham crackers are well worth the effort. They really don't take too much time to prepare, and result in desserts that are extra special.

MAKES ABOUT 20 CRACKERS

*2 tablespoons
granulated sugar*

*½ teaspoon ground cinnamon,
divided*

*4 ounces (1 stick)
unsalted butter, softened*

*¼ cup plus 2 tablespoons
packed light brown sugar*

1 tablespoon honey

1 large egg

¾ cup wheat germ

*1¾ cups unbleached
all-purpose flour*

¼ teaspoon fine sea salt

IN A SMALL bowl, combine the granulated sugar and ¼ teaspoon of the cinnamon.

In the bowl of a stand mixer fitted with the paddle attachment, cream the butter, brown sugar, and honey on the lowest speed until evenly combined but the sugar granules have not dissolved. Add the egg and continue to mix until evenly combined. Add the wheat germ, flour, the remaining ¼ teaspoon cinnamon, and the salt all at once, and mix until the dough is smooth and just comes together in a ball.

Remove the dough from the mixer, divide the dough in half, and flatten each piece into a 1-inch-thick disk. Wrap each disk tightly in plastic wrap and refrigerate until firm, 1 to 2 hours.

Position a rack in the center of the oven and preheat to 350°F. Line two baking sheets with parchment paper.

Between 2 sheets of parchment, roll one disk of dough into a large, ⅛-inch-thick rectangle; return to the refrigerator until firm. Repeat with the remaining disk of dough.

Peel away the parchment paper on one side of the first sheet of dough to loosen it, then place the parchment back over the dough. Flip over the entire sandwich of paper and dough, peel away the parchment on the top of the dough, and discard. Cut the dough into 2½-inch squares and place on the prepared baking sheets about 1 inch apart. Dock gently with a fork and sprinkle with half of the cinnamon-sugar mixture. Repeat with the second sheet of dough.

Bake the crackers until light golden brown, about 8 minutes. Let cool on the baking sheets to room temperature.

NOTE: Graham crackers can be stored in an airtight container for up to 5 days.

VANILLA BEAN CRÊPES

The first time I watched a *crêpier* expertly swirl batter into a paper-thin pancake using a little wooden turning stick on a smoking hot griddle, I was amazed at his skill. Following my uncomplicated instructions for making crêpes, you too, with a bit of practice, can become a master. MAKES 16 CRÊPES

2 large eggs

1 teaspoon pure vanilla extract

¾ cup plus 3 tablespoons unbleached all-purpose flour

¼ cup granulated sugar

1 cup whole milk

1 tablespoon unsalted butter, melted

Nonstick cooking spray

COMBINE THE EGGS, vanilla, flour, sugar, milk, and melted butter in a blender and process until smooth, scraping any dry ingredients from the sides of the blender as needed. Strain the mixture through a fine-mesh sieve into a bowl, then cover and let rest in the refrigerator for 1 hour or up to 2 days.

Line a plate or baking sheet with the parchment paper.

Over high heat, warm an 8-inch nonstick sauté or crêpe pan, lightly coated with nonstick cooking spray, until very hot. Lower the heat to medium, remove the pan from the heat, and ladle about 1 ounce (or 2 tablespoons) of batter into the pan, swirling the batter until it evenly coats the base of the pan. Return the pan to the heat and, as when cooking a pancake, cook the crêpe until small bubbles appear and the surface becomes matte.

Using a small spatula, gently lift the edge of the crêpe, carefully grab it with your fingertips, and quickly flip it over; cook for about 2 more seconds. To remove the crêpe from the pan, simply invert the pan over the prepared baking sheet and lay the crêpe flat to cool. Lightly coat the pan again with nonstick cooking spray and return the pan to the heat for a few seconds to reheat. Repeat the cooking process with the remaining batter, arranging the crêpes on the baking sheet as they are cooked.

For Cocoa Crêpes: Substitute 3 tablespoons cocoa powder for the 3 tablespoons unbleached all-purpose flour.

NOTE: Without a filling, crêpes are best eaten immediately. If filled, let them cool to room temperature and cover with plastic wrap for up to 3 hours before serving.

STREUSEL

I always keep a bit of streusel tucked away in my freezer—it's perfect for a last-minute dessert. I suggest you double this recipe and store half of it for later use. When kept in an airtight container, streusel will easily last two to three months. Don't forget to date the container. MAKES 7 CUPS

3¼ cups unbleached all-purpose flour

¾ cup granulated sugar

¾ cup packed light brown sugar

½ teaspoon ground cinnamon

1½ teaspoons fine sea salt

10 ounces (2½ sticks) unsalted butter, melted and cooled to room temperature

LINE A BAKING sheet with parchment paper.

In a large mixing bowl, stir the flour, granulated sugar, brown sugar, cinnamon, and salt together to combine. Continue to stir and slowly pour in the melted butter. Mix until the mixture just starts to clump together into pea-sized pieces. Spread the streusel on the prepared baking sheet and refrigerate until ready to use.

For Oatmeal Streusel: Stir 1 cup old-fashioned rolled oats into the dry ingredients before adding the melted butter.

CARAMEL SAUCE

Don't be concerned when making this flavorful caramel as it turns a deep brown and appears about to burn. Once you remove the saucepan of caramelized sugar from the heat and add the heavy cream, the sauce will lighten to a tawny brown. MAKES I CUP

½ cup granulated sugar

½ teaspoon fine sea salt

1 tablespoon light corn syrup

1 tablespoon water

½ cup heavy cream

IN A SMALL saucepan, bring the sugar, salt, corn syrup, and water to a boil. Cook until the mixture reaches 365°F on an instant-read candy thermometer. Immediately remove from the heat, add the cream, and whisk until smooth, taking care to avoid any steam and bubbling that may occur as the cream is added to the hot caramel. Transfer the mixture to a heatproof bowl and refrigerate until chilled, about 1 hour.

MILK, SEMISWEET, AND DARK CHOCOLATE GANACHES

In my professional pastry kitchen, a chocolate ganache can be used for a variety of recipes. When warm, try using ganache as a sauce, the base flavoring for drinking chocolate, or a dip for cookies and candies. When chilled, a ganache can be scooped into truffles, or thinned with more cream and whipped into a simple cake or pie filling.

MAKES I CUP

½ cup (about 3 ounces) chocolate chips

3 tablespoons heavy cream

1 tablespoon light corn syrup

PUT THE CHOCOLATE chips in a large heatproof bowl and set aside.

In a small saucepan, bring the cream and corn syrup to a boil. Pour over the chocolate, let stand for 2 minutes, then gently whisk until smooth. Transfer the mixture to a liquid measuring cup with a pour spout and let cool until slightly warmer than room temperature.

For Milk Chocolate Ganache: Use milk chocolate chips and follow the recipe as directed.

For Semisweet Chocolate Ganache: Use semisweet chocolate chips, increase the cream to 4 tablespoons, and follow the recipe as directed.

For Dark Chocolate Ganache: Use dark chocolate chips, increase the cream to 4 tablespoons, and follow the recipe as directed.

HOMEMADE CRÈME FRAÎCHE

Of all the cheeses one can make from scratch, crème fraîche must be the simplest. Stir together two basic ingredients, set them aside for an overnight stay on your kitchen counter, and you'll have something homemade and delicious that can be used for a variety of recipes. MAKES 3 CUPS

3 cups heavy cream

¼ cup buttermilk

WHISK THE CREAM and buttermilk together in a nonreactive bowl, cover with cheesecloth, and let sit out overnight at room temperature. Transfer the crème fraîche to the refrigerator and let chill for 1 day before using.

WHIPPED MASCARPONE

Whipped cream is a wonderful addition to many desserts, but whipped mascarpone is even better because it is richer and more flavorful. Serve it alongside a slice of pie or put a dollop on a piece of cake. It will not disappoint. MAKES ABOUT 3 CUPS

2 cups (8 ounces) mascarpone

½ cup heavy cream

¼ cup confectioners' sugar

Seeds from ½ vanilla bean

IN THE BOWL of a stand mixer fitted with the paddle attachment, cream the mascarpone, cream, confectioners' sugar, and vanilla on medium speed until smooth and just thickened.

For Whipped Lemon Mascarpone: Add the finely grated zest of 1 lemon.

SIMPLE BUTTERCREAM ICING

I call this buttercream icing simple because it is effortless to make. The recipe calls for four basic ingredients. The stand mixer does all the work. The result is a fabulously thick, rich, and creamy frosting that will spread over a layer cake or cupcakes with ease. MAKES 5 TO 6 CUPS

8 large egg whites

1 cup granulated sugar

1 pound (4 sticks) unsalted butter, softened

Pinch of fine sea salt

IN THE BOWL of a stand mixer fitted with the whisk attachment, beat the egg whites and sugar on high speed until thick, glossy, and tripled in volume, about 8 minutes. Reduce the speed of the mixer to low and slowly add the butter, 1 tablespoon at a time, and the salt. Scrape down the sides of the bowl, increase the mixer speed to high, and whip until thickened and completely smooth, about 10 minutes. Set the icing aside at room temperature until ready use, up to 3 hours.

For Malted Milk Buttercream: Once the butter has been added to the icing, but before the sides of the bowl have been scraped down, add ¼ cup barley malt syrup to the mixer. Proceed with the recipe as instructed. Set the icing aside at room temperature until ready use, up to 3 hours.

For Brown Sugar Buttercream: Reduce the amount of granulated sugar in the recipe to ¾ cup and add 1 cup packed light brown sugar to the egg whites. Proceed with the recipe as instructed. Set the icing aside at room temperature until ready use, up to 3 hours.

WHITE ICING

This most basic of icings can be used for a variety of desserts—it can be a glaze for doughnuts, pound cakes, or shortbread cookies. With bits of lemon zest or a few pinches of ground nutmeg, it will dress up many sweets for a special occasion. MAKES 3 CUPS

3 cups confectioners' sugar

¼ cup plus 2 tablespoons whole milk

WHISK THE CONFECTIONERS' sugar and milk together until smooth. Cover with plastic wrap and let stand at room temperature until ready to use, up to 1 hour.

SWEET CREAM ICE CREAM

It is evident from this recipe's many variations that an ice-cream base is nothing more than a vehicle for many ingredients. This base can be steeped with dried spices, chiles, herbs, or tea leaves. Folding chocolate chips, jam, chopped fruit, or nuts into freshly frozen ice cream is also delicious. Whenever possible, use fresh eggs, whole milk, and heavy cream from the farmers' market. Be adventurous—whatever flavor combination you fancy is certain to make an excellent ice cream. MAKES I QUART

6 large egg yolks

1½ cups whole milk

1½ cups heavy cream

¼ teaspoon fine sea salt

½ cup plus 2 tablespoons granulated sugar, divided

PREPARE A LARGE bowl of ice water and set aside.

Put the egg yolks in a large bowl; cover with plastic wrap and set aside. In a medium saucepan, bring the milk, cream, salt, and ¼ cup of the sugar to a full boil. Remove from the heat and set aside.

Whisk the remaining ¼ cup plus 2 tablespoons sugar into the bowl with the yolks until smooth. Gently temper the yolks by slowly adding the hot cream mixture, whisking constantly. When the mixture is completely combined, strain through a fine-mesh sieve into a large bowl. Place the bowl of ice-cream base in the bowl of ice water and stir until cool.

Freeze the mixture in an ice-cream machine according to the manufacturer's directions until the ice cream has a smooth, soft-serve-like texture. Store in the freezer for 4 hours before serving.

For Vanilla Bean Ice Cream: Add the seeds from 1 vanilla bean to the saucepan of milk, cream, salt, and sugar. Bring to a boil, then remove the pan from the heat and let steep for 10 minutes. Return the mixture to a full boil, then proceed with the recipe as instructed.

For Lavender Ice Cream: Add 1 tablespoon fresh or dried lavender flowers and the zest of 1 lemon to the saucepan of milk, cream, salt, and sugar. Bring to a boil, then remove the pan from the heat and let steep for 10 minutes. Return the mixture to a full boil, then proceed with the recipe as instructed.

For Peppermint–Cacao Nib Ice Cream: Add 1 cup fresh peppermint leaves (stems removed) to the saucepan of milk, cream, salt, and sugar. Bring to a boil, then remove the pan from the heat and let steep for 10 minutes. Return the mixture to a full boil, then proceed with the recipe as instructed.

After the ice cream has been frozen in the ice-cream machine, immediately fold ¼ cup cacao nibs into the ice cream, then store in the freezer for 4 hours before serving.

ROASTED SUGAR PUMPKIN AND KABOCHA SQUASH

Combining pumpkin with kabocha squash is one of my autumn baking secrets. Making homemade roasted pumpkin puree is the ideal way to fill a pie, but when the puree is mixed with roasted kabocha squash, which has a thicker texture and stronger flavor, your pumpkin desserts will be extra satisfying. MAKES ABOUT 8 CUPS

One 4-pound sugar pumpkin

One 4-pound kabocha squash

POSITION A RACK in the center of the oven and preheat to 350°F. Cut the pumpkin and squash into eighths; remove and discard the seeds. Place the pumpkin and squash pieces in a large baking dish, fill with about ¼ inch of water, and cover with aluminum foil. Roast for 1 hour to 1 hour and 15 minutes, until the flesh is fork tender.

Remove from the oven and discard the foil. When the pumpkin and the squash pieces are cool enough to handle, use a large spoon to scrape the flesh from the skin; discard the skins. Puree the pumpkin and squash flesh in a food processor until smooth. Let cool to room temperature before refrigerating or using.

NOTE: This recipe makes more puree than called for in any of the recipes in this book. Freeze the leftovers in small containers for up to 3 months and defrost just before using.

RESOURCE GUIDE

Specialty Ingredients

Aperol
www.AperolUSA.com
Aperol liqueur

Bee Raw
95 Greene Street
New York, NY 10012
(888) 660-0090
www.BeeRaw.com
Buckwheat honey and sage honey

Bittersweet Plantation
(800) 256-2433
www.JFolse.com
Creole cream cheese

Bob's Red Mill
13521 S.E. Pheasant Court
Milwaukie, OR 97222
(800) 349-2173
www.BobsRedMill.com
Almond flour, buckwheat flour, flaxseeds, stone-ground cornmeal, wheat germ, and other flours and grains

Buon Italia
75 Ninth Avenue
New York, NY 10011
(212) 633-9090
www.BuonItalia.com
Amaretti cookies, Italian savoiardi ladyfingers, chestnut flour, and other Italian ingredients

The Chef's Warehouse
(718) 842-8700
www.ChefsWarehouse.com
Brandied cherries, Sicilian Bronte pistachios, smoked sea salt, elderflower cordial, and other specialty food items

Coombs Family Farms
P.O. Box 117
Brattleboro, VT 05302
(888) 266-6271
www.CoombsFamilyFarms.com
Grade B maple syrup

Frog Hollow Farm
P.O. Box 2110
Brentwood, CA 94513
(888) 779-4511
www.FrogHollow.com
California's finest pluots, stone fruit, and pears

Goya
100 Seaview Drive
Secaucus, NJ 07094
(201) 348-4900
www.Goya.com
Frozen passion fruit pulp

Hammons
105 Hammons Drive
P.O. Box 140
Stockton, MO 65785
(888) 429-6887
www.Black-Walnuts.com
Black walnuts

Left Hand Brewing Company
1265 Boston Avenue
Longmont, CO 80501
(303) 772-0258
www.LeftHandBrewing.com
Milk stout beer

Mountain Rose Herbs
P.O. Box 50220
Eugene, OR 97405
(800) 879-3337
www.MountainRoseHerbs.com
Hibiscus petals and dried lavender flowers

N.Y. Cake and Bake
56 West 22nd Street
New York, NY 10010
(800) 942-2539
www.NYCake.com
Gold dust, pearl sugar, silver dragées, and other specialty baking ingredients; bakeware, tools, and cake decorating supplies

Nellie and Joe's Famous Lime Juice
(800) 546-3743
www.KeyLimeJuice.com
Key lime juice

Nielsen-Massey
1550 Shields Drive
Waukegan, IL 60085
(800) 525-7873
www.NielsenMassey.com
Almond extract, orange blossom extract, and rose water

Old Chatham Sheepherding Company
155 Shaker Museum Road
Old Chatham, NY 12136
(888) 743-3760
www.BlackSheepCheese.com
Sheep's milk yogurt

Piedmont Distillers
3960 U.S. 220 Highway
Madison, NC 27025
(336) 445-0055
www.CatdaddyMoonshine.com
Catdaddy Spiced Moonshine

Singing Dog Vanilla
P.O. Box 50042
Eugene, OR 97405
(888) 343-0002
www.SingingDogVanilla.com
Bourbon vanilla bean pods, pure vanilla extract, and ground cinnamon

Valrhona
45 Main Street
Brooklyn, NY 11201
(888) 682-5746
www.Valrhona-Chocolate.com
Milk, semisweet, and dark chocolate bars and chips, cacao nibs, and cocoa powder

Whole Foods Market
www.WholeFoodsMarket.com
Almond paste, barley malt syrup, roasted chestnuts, candied orange peel, Dufour puff pastry, instant espresso powder, phyllo dough, pistachio nut paste, puffed brown rice, Zante currants, unsweetened shredded coconut, unsweetened coconut flakes, and other all-natural baking ingredients

Equipment, Tools, and Supplies

ABC Home
888 Broadway
New York, NY 10003
(646) 602-3797
www.ABCHome.com
Tableware, flatware, linens, cookware, and home decor

All-Clad
424 Morganza Road
Canonsburg, PA 15317
(800) 255-2523
www.All-Clad.com
Professional- and home kitchen–quality cookware and bakeware

Fishs Eddy
889 Broadway
New York, NY 10003
(877) 347-4733
www.FishsEddy.com
Tableware, flatware, linens, cookware, and home decor

KitchenAid
P.O. Box 218
Saint Joseph, MI 49085
(800) 541-6390
www.KitchenAid.com
Countertop appliances and bakeware

Nordic Ware
5005 Highway 7
Minneapolis, MN 55416
(877) 466-7342
www.NordicWare.com
Quality Bundt pans and rosette irons

Williams-Sonoma
(877) 812-6235
www.Williams-Sonoma.com
Bakeware, countertop appliances, cookbooks, and gourmet baking ingredients and supplies

ACKNOWLEDGMENTS

To my mother, for always knowing I would accomplish all I set my mind to. I wish you were here to share in the satisfaction of achieving a goal I dreamed up fourteen years ago.

To Simon, who always rolls up his sleeves and jumps into the fire. Thank you for being my sounding board, sharing your level-headed advice and opinions, pushing me to be the best person I can be, washing dishes, and making the cherry jam pie.

To my editor extraordinaire, Sandy Gilbert, who believed in my cookbook concept from the very start. Thank you for allowing me to spread my wings as far as I could stretch, then clipping them in the final hour to actually get this glorious cookbook off to the printer. Working with you has been a real treat, and I look forward to many more books in the future.

To my literary agent, Vicky Bijur. You are one tough cookie, and I can't thank you enough. I appreciate your honesty, your challenge of my many whims, and your insistence upon my writing a book to satisfy more than just my own appetite. I am so pleased you love this book as much as I do. It wouldn't be here without your hard work and dedication.

To my book team: Photographer, Pernille Pedersen—your artistic direction led this project from beginning to end, and your bright and sunny disposition infused its way into every shot. I couldn't be more grateful for such a wonderful person to share half of the pages in this book. Graphic designer, Jan Derevjanik—each page is perfect; your expertise and ease in understanding the look and feel of this book is seen throughout. Prop stylist, Michelle Wong—your aesthetic perfectly framed every dessert, and I envy your style and collection of the most beautiful of things. Amy Wilkinson— your use of cotton swabs and the placement of each little crumb magically highlighted the scrumptiousness in each image. And Junita Bognanni—what in the world would I have done without you? You were the twine that held this baker together throughout the duration of this book. My most heartfelt thanks for your cool, calm, and collected commitment. To the bakers who helped me prep in the kitchen—Onna Hepner, Mia Hutterer, Jess Kantor, Mariko Kondo, Rita Lee, and Danielle Spencer. To the wordsmith team—Liana Krissoff, Deborah Weiss Geline, and Hilary Ney, and indexer Marilyn Flaig—thank you for your finishing touches. Lastly, to Tracey Zabar—I am ever grateful for your sage guidance, which is reflected throughout this book.

To the chefs and professional mentors who shaped and inspired me throughout my career: Emeril Lagasse, Celeste Zeccola, Paul Kahan and Donnie Madia, Karen Page and Andrew Dornenburg, Shane Pritchett, Bill Telepan, Hillary Sterling, Alain Joseph, James Tracey, Katie Grieco, Tom Colicchio, Damon Wise, Marc Forgione, Missy Robbins, Carol Wang, Jessica Cutter, David Lebovitz, Karen DeMasco, Sarabeth Levine, Gale Gand, Christina Tosi, Dorie Greenspan, the faculty at the Institute of Culinary Education, Emily Wollman, David Slater, Bradford Phillips, Don Yamauchi, Charlie Trotter, Tony Cruz, Ed Levine, George Atterbury, Della Gossett, Kate Zuckerman, Emily Luchetti, Alex Espiritu, Nick Malgieri, Claudia Fleming, Antoinette Bruno, Alex Kakoyiannis, Alan Batt, Warren Scheideman, Carol McGury, and David Zabar. Thank you for sharing your wisdom, communities, cookbooks, and kitchens.

To my family: Grandpa Sandy, instead of joining Mensa, I perfected your recipe for Charlotte Russe. Grandma Ruth, the sweetest woman on earth, all the sugar in the world can't match you. Karen Wagner, thank you for your advice in navigating the world of writing and also the depths of my father's mind. Uncle Ben, thanks for always helping me laugh it off. The folks in Alabama, thanks for all the love from afar. Jovana, my very best friend, and the Maniacis, thank you for your unconditional love, being great cheerleaders, and for sharing your pretty collectibles. Jane Kristak, I adore you and thank you for welcoming me into your family as though I've always belonged (and I'm sorry I broke your pie plate).

To my dearest of friends, all of whom contributed in endless ways: Eric Papa, Shuna Lydon, Anya Strzemien, Colin Sterling, Sandra Palmer, Natalie Walsh, Melissa Gorman, Keren Weiner, Mike Stein, Jenni Lane Hart, Erin Allweiss, Kristy Magner, Arianna Petrich, Katie and Joe Pedroza, Frank Relle, Camille Finefrock, Perry Chen, Meredith Petran, and Sarah and Christopher Vandendriessche. I hope all the baked goods were payment enough.

A million and one thanks. I am forever grateful to you all.

INDEX

Page numbers in *italics* indicate illustrations.

U.S. AND METRIC CONVERSION CHARTS

All conversions are approximate.

WEIGHT CONVERSIONS

U.S.	METRIC
½ ounce	14 g
1 ounce	28 g
1½ ounces	43 g
2 ounces	57 g
2½ ounces	71 g
3 ounces	85 g
3½ ounces	100 g
4 ounces	113 g
5 ounces	142 g
6 ounces	170 g
7 ounces	200 g
8 ounces	227 g
9 ounces	255 g
10 ounces	284 g
11 ounces	312 g
12 ounces	340 g
13 ounces	368 g
14 ounces	400 g
15 ounces	425 g
1 pound	454 g

OVEN TEMPERATURES

°F	GAS MARK	°C
250	½	120
275	1	140
300	2	150
325	3	165
350	4	180
375	5	190
400	6	200
425	7	220
450	8	230
475	9	240
500	10	260
550	Broil	290

LIQUID CONVERSIONS

U.S.	METRIC
1 teaspoon	5 ml
1 tablespoon	15 ml
2 tablespoons	30 ml
3 tablespoons	45 ml
¼ cup	60 ml
⅓ cup	75 ml
⅓ cup plus 1 tablespoon	90 ml
⅓ cup plus 2 tablespoons	100 ml
½ cup	120 ml
⅓ cup	150 ml
¾ cup	180 ml
¾ cup plus 2 tablespoons	200 ml

U.S.	METRIC
1 cup	240 ml
1 cup plus 2 tablespoons	275 ml
1¼ cups	300 ml
1⅓ cups	325 ml
1½ cups	350 ml
1⅓ cups	375 ml
1¾ cups	400 ml
1¾ cups plus 2 tablespoons	450 ml
2 cups (1 pint)	475 ml
2½ cups	600 ml
3 cups	725 ml
4 cups (1 quart)	945 ml
	(1,000 ml = 1 liter)

A generous thanks to ABC Home, All-Clad, Fishs Eddy, KitchenAid, Red Ape Cinnamon, Singing Dog Vanilla, and Valrhona for supplying dishes, linens, flatware, bakeware, cookware, countertop appliances, tools, chocolate, cinnamon, and vanilla beans used for the recipe testing and photographs in this book.

The botanical prints (The White Buerrée Pear, Oranger à fruits déprimés, Knight's scarlet fleshed Strawberry, *and* The Red Magdalene Peach) *that appear on pages 4, 14, 66, 118, and 172 have been reprinted with the permission of the Royal Horticultural Society, Lindley Library, London, England.*

First published in the United States
of America in 2013 by Rizzoli
International Publications, Inc.
300 Park Avenue South
New York, New York 10010
www.rizzoliusa.com

Text copyright ©2013 Jenny McCoy

Photography copyright ©2013
Pernille Pedersen
Prop Styling by Michelle Wong
Food Styling by Amy Wilkinson
Recipe Testing by Junita Bognanni

2013 2014 2015 2016 /
10 9 8 7 6 5 4 3 2 1

Printed in China

ISBN 13: 978-0-8478-4101-1

Library of Congress Control Number:
2013939435

Project Editor: Sandra Gilbert
Production: Colin Hough-Trapp
Graphic design by Jan Derevjanik